AF612733

CONGREGATION
FOR INSTITUTES OF CONSECRATED LIFE
AND SOCIETIES OF APOSTOLIC LIFE

Ecclesiæ Sponsæ Imago

Instruction

on the *Ordo virginum*

Print on Demand Edition 2021

On the Cover:

The Assumption of the Mother of God, icon
Casa San Giuseppe, Zogno (Bergamo), Italia
© Annalisa Vigani

00120 Città del Vaticano
Tel. 0669845780
e-mail: commerciale.lev@spc.va
www.libreriaeditricevaticana.va
www.vatican.va

ISBN 978-88-266-0648-4

INTRODUCTION

1. The image of the Church as the Bride of Christ is presented in the New Testament as an effective icon, revealing the intimate nature of the relationship that the Lord Jesus wanted to establish with the community of those who believed in him (*Ep* 5:23-32; *Rev* 19:7-9; 21:2-3,9)

Since apostolic times this expression of the mystery of the Church has been demonstrated in a unique way in the lives of those women who with spousal love are dedicated to the Lord Jesus in virginity. Responding to a charism kindled in them by the Holy Spirit, they experience the spiritual fertility of an intimate relationship with him and offer the fruits of this relationship to the Church and to the world.

2. Some passages in the New Testament and in the writings of the first Christian centuries show that this form of evangelical life appeared in a spontaneous way in the different regions where ecclesial communities developed[1]. In the context of pagan society, it took its place among other forms of the ascetic life which were clear signs of the novelty of Christianity and of its capacity to respond to the deepest questions about the meaning of human existence[2]. In a process similar to that which concerned the status of widows who chose continence « in honour of the flesh of the Lord »[3], consecrated female virginity gradually assumed the characteristics of a state of life publicly recognised by the Church[4].

[1] Among the earliest evidence, the testimony of Clement of Rome (CLEMENS ROMANUS, *Ep. Ad Corinthios* 38, 2: *SCh* 167,162) and Ignatius of Antioch (IGNATIUS ANTIOCHENSIS, *Ep. Ad Smyrnenses* XIII: *PG* 5, 717-718; *Ep. Ad Polycarpum* V, 2: *PG* 5, 723-724).

[2] About the year 150, Justinian expressed himself thus: "Many are the men and women who were made disciples of Christ as babies, who remained pure right up to their sixtieth or seventieth years. And I am proud to be able to cite examples coming from all social classes"; JUSTINUS, *Apol. pro christ.*, c. 15: *PG* 6, 349. Athenagoras of Athens, in the year 177 wrote to Marcus Aurelius: "You could find many of ours, men and women, who have grown old without marrying, in the hope of uniting themselves more closely with God!": ATHENAGORAS ATHENIENSE, *Legatio pro christianis* XXXII: *OTAC* VII, 172.

[3] IGNATIUS ANTIOCHENSIS, *Ep. ad Polycarpum* V, 2: *PG* 5, 723-724.

[4] Initially, the similarity between this form of life and that of consecrated widows also entailed a lack of clear distinction, as can be gathered from the writings of Ignati-

In the first three centuries, large numbers of consecrated virgins underwent martyrdom in order to remain faithful to the Lord. Among these were Agatha of Catania, Lucy of Syracuse, Agnes and Cecilia of Rome, Thecla of Iconium, Apollonia of Alexandria, Restituta of Carthage, and Justa and Rufina of Seville. From that time, right up to today the memory of the virgin martyrs has remained as a striking reminder of the total gift of self that virginal consecration demands.

In the women who embraced this vocation and responded to it with a decision to persevere in life-long virginity, the Fathers of the Church saw a reflection of the image of the Church as the Bride, totally dedicated to her Bridegroom: thus they refer to them as *sponsae Christi* (brides of Christ), *Christo dicatae* (dedicated to Christ), *Christo maritatae* (married to Christ), *Deo nuptae* (brides of God)[5]. In the living body of the Church, they com-

us of Antioch, who, at the beginning of the second century, greeted "the virgins called widows" of the community of Smyrna: IGNATIUS ANTIOCHENSIS, *Ep. Ad. Smyrn.* XIII: *PG* 5, 717-718. In the Apostolic Constitutions of the second half of the fourth century, virgins appear together with widows and deaconesses, as an institutional component of the Christian community.

[5] Cf. e.g. ATHANASIUS, *Apol. Ad Constant.* 33: *PG* 25, 640; AMBROSIUS, *De virginibus*, lib. I, c. 8, n. 52: *PL* 16, 202.

prised an institutionalised *coetus* (group), identified by the name of the *Ordo virginum* (Order of virgins)[6].

3. From the IV century, entry into the *Ordo virginum* took place through a solemn liturgical rite presided over by the diocesan bishop. In the heart of the community gathered for the Eucharistic celebration, the woman expressed her *sanctum propositum* (holy resolution) to remain in virginity for her whole life, for the love of Christ. The Bishop then pronounced the consecratory prayer. As affirmed already in the writings of Ambrose of Milan and subsequently, starting from the most ancient liturgical sources, the nuptial symbolism of the rite was displayed particularly by the bestowal of the veil on the virgin by the Bishop, a gesture that corresponded to the *velatio* (placing of the marriage veil) that took place during the marriage celebration[7].

4. The respect and pastoral concern that accompanied the evolution of the consecrat-

[6] This expression is found in BASILIUS, *Ep. 199 Ad Amphilochium*: *PG* 32, 717.

[7] Cf. AMBROSIUS, *De virginibus*, lib. III, cc. 1-3, nn. 1-14: *PL* 16, 219-224; *De institutione virginis*, c. 17, nn. 104-114: *PL* 16, 333-336. Cf. *Sacramentarium Leonianum* XXX: *PL* 55, 129.

ed virgins are amply demonstrated in patristic literature. The Fathers did not limit themselves to criticizing the behaviour of consecrated women that was not in accord with their commitment to lead a chaste life in humble discipleship of Christ. They also challenged and vigorously opposed the arguments of those who denied the value of consecrated virginity as well as heretical deviations that supported the ideal of virginity and continence on the basis of a negative conception of matrimony and sexuality. Reflecting on the theological foundations of virginal consecration, they highlighted its charismatic origins, evangelical motivation, ecclesial and social significance, reference to the Virgin Mary as exemplar, and the prophetic value of anticipation and vigilant expectation of full communion with the Lord that will be brought about only at his glorious return at the end of time. Addressing the consecrated virgins «more with affection than with the authority»[8] of their office, they exhorted consecrated virgins to nourish and express their love for Christ the Bridegroom through attentive meditation on the Scriptures and in persevering personal and liturgical prayer; by practising asceticism, the virtues and the

[8] Cyprianus, *De habitu virginum* III: *PL* 4, 443.

works of mercy; by cultivating an attitude of obedient attention to the magisterium of the Bishop and in the obligation to safeguard ecclesial communion. Thus, they would offer a transparent and persuasive evangelical witness within the Christian community and in the social setting within which they remained inserted, generally living with their family of origin and at times in community.

In the same period, by means of papal decrees and the constitutions of provincial councils, the regulation of essential aspects of this form of life began to be defined.

5. While consecrated virgins in the first centuries usually lived with their own families, as cenobitic monasticism developed the Church associated virginal consecration with community life, and therefore with the observance of a common rule and obedience to a superior. Over the course of centuries, the original way of life of the *Ordo virginum*, with its characteristic foundations in the local ecclesial community under the guidance of the diocesan bishop, gradually disappeared.

The rituals of entrance into monastic life accompanied, and in the majority of monasteries, replaced the celebration of the rite for the *consecratio virginum* (consecration of virgins). Only some monastic families in which solemn vows were made maintained the use of this rite. While preserving the essential elements of the original structure, the rite became enriched with contributions from the culture of the populations among which it spread, through successive revisions that led to the introduction of new prayer formulae and symbolic gestures.

6. The stimulus for ecclesial renewal that inspired the Second Vatican Council also created interest in the liturgical rite for the *consecratio virginum* and in the *Ordo virginum.* Many centuries after its disappearance, and in a radically transformed historical context, in which profound changes in the condition of women in the Church and in society were taking place, this ancient form of consecrated life displayed a surprising force of attraction. It seemed capable of responding not only to the desires of many women to dedicate themselves totally to the Lord and to their neighbours, but also to the concurrent rediscovery by the particular Church of its own identity in communion with the one Body of Christ.

In accordance with the provisions of the Constitution on the Liturgy, *Sacrosanctum concilium* n. 80, in the post-conciliar period the rite for the *consecratio virginum* then in the

Roman Pontifical underwent revision, based on the general principles for the liturgical reform established by the Council. The new *Ordo consecrationis virginum*, promulgated on 31 May 1970 by the Sacred Congregation for Divine Worship on the special mandate of Pope Paul VI, came into force on 6 January 1971[9]. Recovering the most ancient ecclesial tradition, and taking into account its subsequent historical evolution, two forms of celebration were composed and approved. The first is intended for women living *in saeculo* (in the world), that is, in their ordinary circumstances of life, who are admitted to consecration by the diocesan Bishop. The second form is for nuns living in communities in which the rite is used, who are already perpetually professed or who make perpetual profession in the same celebration in which they receive the *consecration virginum.*

7. In this way, virginal consecration has again found explicit ecclesial recognition for women who remain in their ordinary context of life, rooted in the diocesan community, gathered around the Bishop in the manner

[9] *Pontificale Romanum ex decreto Sacrosancti Concilii Œcumenici Vaticani II instauratum auctoritate Pauli PP. VI promulgatum, Ordo consecrations virginum,* Editio typica, Typis Polyglottis Vaticanis, Civitas Vaticana 1970.

of the ancient *Ordo virginum*, without being ascribed to an Institute of consecrated life. The same liturgical text and the norms established in them outline in their essential elements the structure and discipline of this form of consecrated life. Its institutional character – distinctive and different from that of Institutes of consecrated life – has been successively confirmed in the *Code of Canon Law* (can. 604). Similarly, the Code of Canons of the Oriental Churches has explained the possibility that in the Eastern Churches, their own law constitutes consecrated virgins who publicly profess chastity in the world « on their own account », that is, without bonds of belonging to an Institute of consecrated life (can. 570).

As a consequence, in the reorganisation of the Roman Curia that took place according to the Apostolic Constitution *Pastor Bonus*, the *Ordo virginum* was situated within the competence of the Congregation for Institutes of consecrated life and Societies of apostolic life[10].

The Catechism of the Catholic Church[11], the reflections that took place on the occa-

[10] John Paul II, Apostolic Constitution *Pastor bonus* (28 June 1988), 105.

[11] *Catechism of the Catholic Church*, 922-924.

sion of the Synod of Bishops on the theme «Consecrated Life and its Mission in the Church and in the World» and the post-synodal apostolic exhortation *Vita consecrata*[12] (in particular n. 7 and n. 42), have contributed to a clarification of the ecclesial position of the *Ordo virginum* among the other forms of consecrated life, emphasizing the special link that has been established between consecrated virgins and the particular and universal Church.

The Instruction *Starting Afresh from Christ: A renewed commitment to consecrated life in the third millennium*[13], has therefore underlined the need for the diocesan Bishop and his presbyterate to pay special attention to consecrated virgins.

Subsequently the Directory for the pastoral ministry of Bishops, *Apostolorum Successores*[14], in continuity with the ancient ecclesial tradition, reaffirmed that the diocesan

[12] John Paul II, Post-Synodal Apostolic Exhortation *Vita consecrata* (25 March 1996).

[13] Congregation for Institutes of Consecrated Life and Societies of Apostolic Life, Instruction *Starting afresh from Christ. A renewed commitment to consecrated life in the third millennium* (19 May 2002), 19.

[14] Congregation for Bishops, Directory for the Pastoral Ministry of Bishops *Apostolorum Successores* (22 February 2004), 104.

Bishop must take particular interest in the *Ordo virginum*, because these virgins are consecrated to God at his hands and are entrusted to his pastoral care.

8. Since this form of consecrated life was re-introduced in the Church, there has been a real revival of the *Ordo virginum*, whose vitality is evident in the rich variety of personal charisms placed at the service of the Church's development and of the renewal of society in the spirit of the Gospel. The phenomenon appears to be very significant, not only for the number of women involved, but also for its diffusion throughout all continents, in many countries and Dioceses and in very diverse geographic areas and cultural contexts.

Without doubt, the translation of the Latin text of the *Ordo consecrationis virginum* in the majority of modern languages, under the supervision of the respective episcopal conferences, has contributed to this revival.

Large numbers of Bishops have promoted and supported the *Ordo virginum* in their Dioceses through their own teaching and pastoral activity. They encourage the contribution of the consecrated virgins themselves, who hear the call to reflect on their own experience, on the relevance of this vocation in the Church and in today's world and on the attention necessary to enable them to express themselves according to its particular character. With the same purpose, some episcopal conferences have drawn up common criteria and guidelines for the pastoral care of the *Ordo virginum.*

In synergy with the magisterium and the action of the diocesan bishops, the Apostolic See has continued to pay attention to the *Ordo virginum,* putting itself at the service of the particular Churches, to promote the rebirth and development of this way of life in accordance with its special characteristics.

9. The service of communion that the successor of Peter carries out with respect to the *Ordo virginum* was particularly evident on the occasion of the first two international meetings in Rome, which were attended by consecrated virgins from numerous countries. From St. John Paul II in 1995[15] and Benedict XVI in 2008[16], consecrated virgins

[15] John Paul II, *Speech to the participants in the International Conference of the* Ordo virginum *on the 25th anniversary of the promulgation of the rite,* Rome (2 June 1995).

[16] Benedict XVI, *Speech to the participants at the Congress of the* Ordo virginum *on the theme: « Consecrated virginity in the world: a gift for the Church and in the Church »,* Rome (15 May 2008).

received valuable instruction to guide them on their way.

A third international meeting took place in 2016, when consecrated virgins from the entire world were invited to Rome to take part in the final day of the *Year of Consecrated Life* announced by Pope Francis. Under the leadership of the successor of Peter, who has urged consecrated persons in every form of life to rediscover the common foundations of consecrated life, it became evident how the characteristic insertion of the *Order of virgins* in the particular Churches is harmonized with the experience of communion that consecrated virgins encounter within the sphere of the universal Church, enabling them to participate in the one ecclesial mission.

10. In recent years, requests have reached this Dicastery from many places to provide instructions to guide the action of diocesan Bishops in applying the norms in the Roman Pontifical which are implicitly referenced in can. 604 of the *Code of Canon Law*, as well as to draw up more comprehensive, structured regulations, with specific reference to the particularities of the *Ordo virginum*, based on principles common to the law of consecrated life in all its different forms.

The renewed presence of this form of consecrated life in the Church, whose reappearance is so closely linked to the event of the Second Vatican Council, and the rapidity of its growth in so many particular Churches, makes it appropriate to respond to these requests, so that in the necessary adaptations to different cultural contexts, the specific identity of the *Ordo virginum* might be safeguarded.

This Instruction establishes the normative principles and directive criteria that the Pastors of every Diocese and individual Churches assimilated to the Dioceses must apply in the pastoral care of the *Ordo virginum.*

After outlining the biblical foundations and typical elements of the vocation and witness of consecrated virgins (First Part), the Instruction deals with the specific structure of the *Ordo virginum* within the particular Church and the universal Church (Second Part). It then focuses on vocational discernment, formation programs prior to consecration and permanent formation (Third Part).

I.
THE VOCATION AND WITNESS OF THE *ORDO VIRGINUM*

The biblical foundations of consecrated virginity

11. *Be fruitful and multiply* is the command addressed by the Creator to the first couple (*Gen* 1:28) and reaffirmed to Noah and his sons (*Gen* 9:1,7). This command deeply permeated the Hebraic mentality and the whole fabric of the Old Testament. It is connected to the promise of numerous descendants and the fulfilment of the messianic times. Marriage, possibly enriched by children, therefore emerges as the ideal profile of every pious Israelite and a different lifestyle is foreign to the biblical mentality.

In the Pentateuch and the historical books, sexual abstention is required only as a temporary condition of detachment from the profane, in order to enter the sphere of what is associated with God's sanctity: for example, in preparation for meeting the Lord at Sinai (*Ex* 19:15) or for war against the Lord's enemies (*1 Sam* 21:2-7), for the Levites during their cultic service (*Lev* 22:1-9) or to be able to share in a sacred meal (*1 Sm* 21:5). Virginity is valued as a positive quality only in relation to future marriage, and with explicit reference to the condition of the woman (*Deut.* 22:13-21), because it represents the intimacy reserved to the spouses. In particular, the high priest is required to marry a virgin for reasons of ritual purity (*Lev* 21:10-14). Perpetual virginity on the other hand was considered a severe humiliation (see the daughter of Jephthah in *Judg.* 11:37), while physical sterility is endured with much anguish (see Rachel in *Gn* 30:23, Anna in *1 Sm* 1:11 and Elizabeth in *Lk* 1:25).

12. In the wisdom literature, the exaltation of married love (that reached its poetic summit in the *Song of Songs*) is based on the ideal of family life inherited from tradition. Its beauty is admired (e.g. in *Ps* 127:3-5; 128:1-3; *Sir* 25:1) and it is viewed from a moral and pedagogical perspective (e.g. *Prov.* 5:15-19, *Sir* 7:23-28; 9:1,9). Virginity is valued as a virtue in a woman, to be guarded and respected in view of marriage, because it is a proof of her rectitude and of the honour of her family (*Job* 31:1; *Sir* 9:5; 42:10) to the point that, personifying divine Wisdom, the book of Sirach portrays it as a virgin bride who gives herself to one who fears the Lord (*Sir* 15:2). And since virtue is pleasing to God, the insight emerges that there is a spiritual fertility in good works that liberates from mortality even the sterile woman who is unable to establish a family and who has no descendants (*Wis* 3:13-14; 4:1).

13. Beginning with the preaching of Hosea – closely linked to his personal experience of suffering – the spousal metaphor appears in the prophetic books to emphasise the total gratuity of election and God's untiring fidelity to the covenant (*Hos* 1-2; *Ezr* 16; 23), while the people yield to the seduction of other divinities and their rituals. In this symbolic context, the entire people of God are frequently compared to or personified by the image of a virgin, now to denounce the idolatry that exposes them to the risk of perishing, like a virgin who dies without descendants (*Am* 5:2); now to give voice to a lament over their ruin (*Lam* 2:13); now to invite them to repentance (*Jer* 31:21). But sometimes the image is used to proclaim the promise of redemption, with which God will rescue Israel from devastation and abandonment, to rediscover the joy of knowing that he is loved with eternal love (*Jer* 31:4,13; *Is* 62:5).

Even the celibacy of Jeremiah – the only one whom God explicitly ordered not to take a wife – represents a prophetic sign of the punishment that is about to destroy his people (*Jer* 16:2). He is an eloquent instrument of the word of God, a symbol of death, or rather a sorrowful personification of his message of judgement, announcing imminent destruction as a punishment for the people's infidelity to God.

14. In rabbinic thought, the celibate is considered a man *without help, without joy, without blessing* (*Bereshit Rabba* 17:2), likened to *one who sheds blood* or who diminishes the divine image (Treatise *Yevamoth* of the *Babylonian Talmud* 63b). Nevertheless, some exceptions appear among the rabbis and some religious groups such as the Essenes and Healers and in the famous Qumran community.

On the threshold of the New Testament, the figure of John the Baptist is introduced, defining himself as *the friend of the Bridegroom* (*Jn* 3:29). With his ascetic life and preaching he prepared for the coming of the Messiah and the sudden appearance of the Kingdom of God.

15. In the New Testament, the celibate enters onto the scene and is presented as the incarnate prophecy of the *already* and the *not yet* of the Kingdom of God that draws its origin and its own essential purpose from the novelty of the coming of the Kingdom into history. From the time that the Kingdom of God in the Gospels is identified with the preaching, works and the actual person of Jesus, the motivation of celibacy takes on a strongly Christocentric character. The infancy Gospels of Matthew (1:18-25) and above all of Luke (1:26-38) present the newness of the virginity (*carnis et cordis*) of the mother of Jesus, a visible sign of the invisible incarnation of the Son of God and a spousal expression of the covenant with God, to which all believers are called. In addition, the Gospels show Jesus as an itinerant preacher, free of all ties (*Mt* 8:19-20), who displays the imminence of the Kingdom already present and calls for faith and conversion. In fact, the itinerant style of Jesus entails a constant distancing from places and persons. It is not adapted to the needs of family life, where the concerns of one member are closely connected to the concerns of all the other members, giving rise to a strong solidarity and to family politics.

While there are various references to relatives of Jesus, there is never any hint of a wife or children in the Gospels (*Mk* 3:31-32;

6:3; *Jn* 6:42; *Acts* 1:14). Jesus, in fact called his disciples *sons* or *boys* (*tékna, Mk* 10:24; *teknía, Jn* 13:33; *paidía, Jn* 21:5), touching the reality of a spiritual type of sonship. On the occasion when his family came to him to see him (*Mt* 12:47; *Mk* 3:31; *Lk* 8:20) or rather, to take hold of him to bring him back home (*Mk* 3:21), he announced the establishment of his new family, one not based on blood ties, but on a spiritual reality expressed through the desire to carry out the will of God (*Mt* 12:50; *Mk* 3:31-35) or to hear the word of the Lord and put it into practice (*Lk* 8:21). This further birth or rebirth in the Spirit, which goes beyond flesh and blood, is asserted also in John's Prologue (*Jn* 1:12-13) and on the occasion of the dialogue between Jesus and Nicodemus (*Jn* 3:3-8).

Jesus freely embraced a life without family ties and obligations, so that he could dedicate himself totally to the proclamation of the Kingdom and to the fulfilment of the Father's plan of love for humanity. The radical freedom from attachments that Jesus incarnated, he also required of those who followed him, He asked them to *leave* (*afíemi,* in all three synoptics) *everything* (*panta*: *Mt* 19:27; *Mk* 10:28) or *possessions* (*ta idia*: intimate things, one's own area of intimacy, *Lk* 18:28). This also included leaving behind parents, brothers and sisters, as well as wife (*gynḗ*: *Lk* 18:29) or children (*tékna*: *Mt* 19:29; *Mk* 10:29; *Lk* 18:29). To his disciples he spoke of *eunuchia* as an absolutely new condition, understood not as mortification or a contemptuous attitude towards women, but as a particular gift given by God to those who are called to it.

This recalls the famous *logion*: *Not everyone can accept this teaching, but only those to whom it is given* (*Mt* 19:11). From the grammatical point of view, the expression *to whom it is given* (*dédotai*) is equivalent to a divine passive, and means: *those to whom God has granted it*. Only those who enter into comprehension of the mystery of the Kingdom inaugurated by Christ are capable of understanding this gift. It requires a voluntary, free choice and motivation of a theological and eschatological order, being *for the Kingdom of heaven* (*Mt* 19:12).

Celibacy is thus presented as a free choice that takes place in the relational space that is the body. With this choice the person responds to the God of love who calls and reveals himself in the face of Christ[17]. This is

[17] «The words of Christ (*Mt* 19:11-12) originate from all the realism of the human situation and with the same realism they lead him beyond, towards the call. In a new way,

not a flight from relationship, nor is it the fruit of superhuman force, but a gift that belongs to the dynamism of the transfiguration of relationality that distinguishes the style begun by Jesus: evangelical fraternity, the basis of reconciled humanity and the foundation of *koinōnía* on which the life of the Church is based[18].

while remaining through his nature a "dual" being (that is directed as man towards the woman, and as woman, towards the man), he is able to discover in this solitude, which does not cease being a personal dimension of the duality of each one, a new and even fuller form of intersubjective communication with others. This orientation of the call explains in an explicit way the expression: "For the Kingdom of heaven". In fact, the fulfilment of this Kingdom must be found along the lines of an authentic development of the image and likeness of God, in his Trinitarian significance, which is precisely "in communion". In choosing continence for the Kingdom of heaven, man has the self-awareness to be able, in this way, to fulfil himself "differently" and, in a certain sense, "more" than in marriage, becoming "a sincere gift for others"»: John Paul II, *Audience* (7 April 1982).

[18] «Continence "for the Kingdom of heaven", the choice of virginity or celibacy for one's whole life, in the experience of the disciples and the followers of Christ becomes a particular act of response to the love of the Divine Bridegroom. It therefore has acquired the significance of an act of spousal love, which is a spousal self-giving, for the purpose of reciprocating in a special way the spousal love of the Redeemer; self-giving, understood as renunciation, but done above all for love»: John Paul II, *Audience* (28 April 1982).

The proclamation of the Kingdom opens up to the disciples a new eschatological situation, to which everything else takes second place (*Mt* 10:37; *Lk* 14:26; *Mt* 19:27-29; *Mk* 10:28-30; *Lk* 18:29). In *Mt* 22:23-33, *Mk* 12:18-27 and *Lk* 20:27-40, reference to the eschatological condition of those who have been raised from the dead shows how the choice of celibacy and virginity for the sake of Christ and the Gospel already places the disciples – with a symbolic anticipatory function – in the reality of the Kingdom[19].

[19] «The human being, male and female [...] with free will chooses continence "for the sake of the Kingdom of heaven" [...] indicating [...] the eschatological "virginity" of the risen man, in which will be revealed the absolute and eternal spousal significance of the glorified body in union with God himself, by seeing him "face to face"; and glorified, also, by the union of a perfect intersubjectivity, which will unite all the "participants in the other world", men and women, in the mystery of the communion of saints. Earthly continence "for the Kingdom of heaven" is undoubtedly a sign which points to this truth and this reality. It is a sign that the body, whose end is not death, reaches towards glorification and is already, in itself, I would say, among men a witness that anticipates the future resurrection. Nevertheless, this charismatic sign of the *other world* expresses the strength and the most authentic dynamic of the mystery of the "redemption of the body": a mystery that from Christ has been written in the earthly history of man and has been deeply rooted in this history. Thus continence "for the Kingdom of heaven" bears above all the imprint of the likeness of Christ, who himself made

16. Writing to the Corinthians, Paul placed marriage side by side with virginity, presenting it not in the tone of a command, but as *a recommendation* (*1 Cor* 7:25), a personal call from God, or *a charism* (*1 Cor* 7:7). He characterizes it as a state of life that permits greater dedication to the Lord (*1 Cor* 7:32-35), a witness that Christians do not belong to this world, a sign of the Church straining towards its final goal, and an anticipation of the resurrected state (*1 Cor* 7:29,31). The accent is not on the physical state, but on the total dedication of the person to Christ and to service for the Kingdom. In this sense, in the eyes of Paul, the community itself is the *virgin* that he, as the father, has betrothed to Christ, so that, keeping intact the faith aroused by the apostolic preaching, it might direct all its energies and dedication to him (*2 Cor* 11:2-4).

In the heavenly Jerusalem all the elect are called *virgins* (*Rev* 14:4), to express their fidelity to the covenant and their being uncontaminated by idols. In the book of Revelation virginity appears as a sign of recognition of belonging to the heavenly city, to the bride of the Lamb (*Rev* 21:2,9).

the same choice "for the Kingdom of heaven" in his work of redemption»: JOHN PAUL II, *Audience* (24 March 1982).

If Jesus, the consecrated one par excellence, lives his consecration not in terms of separation from the profane or impure, in fulfilment of legal prescriptions, but by accepting the body that the Father had given him and by giving himself on the cross, his body is the actual place and the effective sign of his consecration to his Father's plan (*Heb* 10:5-10). So it will be also for all who set foot on the path of celibacy or virginity: the body becomes a word, announcing their total belonging to the Lord and their joyful service of their brothers and sisters.

17. Christian virginity thus exists in the world as a clear sign of the future Kingdom because its presence exposes the relativity of material goods and the transitory nature of the world itself. In this sense, like the celibacy of the prophet Jeremiah, it foretells the imminent end. But at the same time, because of the spousal bond with Christ, it also proclaims the beginning of the life of the world to come, the new world according to the Spirit. This sign, as occurs in the biblical vision, is not a simply conventional reference or the pale image of a distant reality, but the reality itself in its nascent expression. In the sign is contained, even if still hidden, the future reality.

Consecrated virginity is therefore placed in a spousal framework, which is not theogamic (meaning: of marriage with the divinity), but theologal, that is, baptismal, because it concerns the spousal love of Christ for the Church (cf. *Eph* 5:25-26). It concerns a supernatural salvific reality, not just a human one, that cannot be explained with the logic of reason but with faith, because, as the scriptures call to mind, *Your husband is your creator* (*Is* 54:5). This is one of the *great works* of the new order inaugurated with Christ's Passover and the outpouring of the Spirit, an experience difficult for *carnal* humanity to understand and comprehensible only by those who let themselves be taught by the Spirit of God (cf. *1 Cor* 2:12-13).

Charism and Vocation

18. Women in whom the Spirit inspires the charism of virginity (*Mt* 19:11-12) receive the grace of a special vocation, with which God the Father draws them to the heart of the nuptial covenant (*Rev* 19:7-9) which, in his eternal plan of love he wanted to establish with humanity and which is fulfilled in the incarnation and the paschal experience of the Son.

This is the *great mystery* (*Eph* 5:32) that is brought about in the Church, the Bride for whom Christ has given himself, in order to make her holy and without blemish (*Eph* 5:25-27), the sacrament of the communion of God with the people[20]. From this nuptial mystery, in which all the baptised are immersed, Christian spouses receive the grace of the sacrament that strengthens them in their union (*Eph* 5:28-29).

Because of their particular vocation, those women who receive virginal consecration in the Church also draw on this mystery. For love of Christ, who is supremely loved, they renounce the experience of human matrimony to be united with him with a spousal bond, to experience and to give witness in the virginal condition (*1 Cor* 7:34) to the fruitfulness of this union, anticipating the reality of definitive communion with God to which all humanity is called (*Lk* 20:34-36).

The *propositum*, the consecration and the state of life

19. This spiritual reality is signified and effected in the liturgical celebration of the *consecratio virginum*, in which the Church

[20] Cf. Second Vatican Ecumenical Council, Dogmatic Constitution on the Church *Lumen gentium*, 1.

prays for God's grace and the outpouring of the Holy Spirit on the virgins[21].

In the rite, those to be consecrated express the *sanctum propositum* (the holy resolution). This is the firm and definitive resolve to persevere for their whole life in perfect chastity, and in the service of God and the Church, following Christ in accordance with the Gospel, to give the world a living witness of love and to be a clear sign of the future Kingdom[22].

The *propositum* of those to be consecrated is accepted and confirmed by the Church through the solemn prayer of the Bishop, who invokes and obtains for them the spiritual anointing that establishes the spousal bond with Christ and consecrates them to God under a new title[23].

In this way, these virgins become consecrated persons, a sublime sign of the love of the Church for Christ and an eschatological image of the heavenly bride and of the life to come[24]. Their exclusive belonging

[21] Cf. *Ordo consecrationis virginum, Prænotanda,* 1; *Catechismus Catholicæ Ecclesiæ,* 1667-1672; *Code of Canon Law,* cann. 1166-1169.

[22] Cf. *Ordo consecrationis virginum,* 17 and 22-23.

[23] Cf. *Ordo consecrationis virginum, Prænotanda,* 1; *Ordo consecrationis virginum,* 16, 24.

[24] Cf. *Ordo consecrationis virginum, Prænotanda,* 1.

to Christ, ratified by the nuptial bond, nourishes in them a vigilant expectation of the return of the glorious bridegroom (*Mt* 25:1-13). It associates them in a particular way with his redemptive sacrifice and dedicates them to the development of the Church and to its mission in the world (*Col* 1:24).

20. The nature of the Church is reflected in the life of consecrated virgins. It is animated as much by charity as by contemplation and action; it is disciple and missionary; it yearns for eschatological fulfilment and at the same time shares the joys and the hopes, the griefs and the anxieties of the people of this age[25], especially those who are the most fragile or poor; it is immersed in the mystery of divine transcendence and incarnate in the history of humanity.

For this reason, consecration establishes a special relationship of communion with both the particular and the universal Church[26]. This is defined by a distinct bond that determines the acquisition of a new

[25] Cf. Second Vatican Ecumenical Council, Pastoral Constitution on the Church in the Modern World, *Gaudium et Spes*, 1.

[26] Cf. John Paul II, Post-Synodal Apostolic Exhortation *Vita consecrata* (25 March 1996), 7 and 42.

state of life and admits them into the *Ordo virginum*[27].

The institutional configuration and pastoral care of this form of life therefore requires the mediation of the ministry of the diocesan Bishop, or in a particular Church equivalent to a Diocese[28], the ministry of the pastor who presides over it, in communion with the Successor of Peter.

The spiritual features

21. The vocation of virgins consecrated in the *Ordo virginum*, like every Christian vocation, is the experience of dialogue between divine grace and human freedom. In fact, the virgin's self-dedication is preceded, sustained and brought to fulfilment by the free, gratuitous initiative of God, on the basis of the baptismal vocation and within the generative fraternal framework of ecclesial relationships[29]. This can only be understood, therefore, from the starting point of the radical unity of the people of God, derived from the one Spirit and founded on the apostles,

[27] Cf. *Code of Canon Law*, can. 604

[28] Cf. *Code of Canon Law*, can. 368 and can. 381 § 2.

[29] Cf. John Paul II, Post-Synodal Apostolic Exhortation *Vita consecrata* (25 March 1996), 14.

resplendent with its variety of charisms and ministries, all complementary and all able to contribute to the one mission of the Church (*Rm* 12:4-5).

22. As in the most ancient ecclesial tradition, the spiritual appearance of consecrated women belonging to the *Ordo virginum* is distinguished by its foundation in the particular Church gathered around the Bishop as the pastor. This feature is portrayed especially in the rite of consecration, in which the primary reference is the model of the Church: a virgin, for the integrity of the faith; a spouse, for the indissoluble union with Christ; and a mother, for the multitude of children born into the life of grace[30].

Virginity, the married state and motherhood[31] are three perspectives that facilitate the description of the spiritual experience of consecrated virgins. They do not refer to juxtaposed or aggregated characteristics, but to spiritual energies that validate each other. They are inscribed in the fundamental coordinates of baptismal life, through which consecrated women are daughters of the Church

[30] Cf. *Ordo consecrationis virginum*, 16.

[31] Cf. JOHN PAUL II, Apostolic Letter *Mulieris dignitatem* (15 August 1988), 17-20.

and sisters connected to all men and women by the bonds of fraternity.

23. The virginity of consecrated women has its foundation and meaning in the faith of the Church. Indeed it is lived in the light of Christ and for love of him, and refers to the integral acceptance, without limitation or compromise, of the Trinitarian revelation that is fulfilled definitively in him[32]. In virginity they express their total trust in the Lord Jesus, which reaches the person at the heart of her humanity, in her original solitude, just where the image and likeness of God is indelibly imprinted and where, despite every fall and wound of sin, life can be renewed in accordance with the Spirit. The charism of virginity, accepted by the woman and confirmed by the Church through consecration, is a gift that derives from the Father, by means of the Son, in the Spirit. This gift safeguards, puri-

[32] «The chastity of celibates and virgins, as a manifestation of dedication to God with an undivided heart (cf. *1 Cor* 7:32-34), is a reflection of the infinite love which links the three Divine Persons in the mysterious depths of the life of the Trinity»: John Paul II, Post-synodal Apostolic Exhortation *Vita consecrata* (25 March 1996), 21. «The integrity of the faith was also tied to the image of the Church as a virgin and her fidelity in love for Christ her spouse; harming the faith means harming communion with the Lord»: Francis, Encyclical Letter *Lumen fidei* (29 June 2013), 48.

fies, heals and increases the capacity of the person to love. It draws back into unity every fragment of her history and the various dimensions of her humanity – spirit, soul and body –, so that she might be able to respond to this grace with the undivided, free and joyful commitment of her own existence.

24. Thus Christian virginity is an experience of spousal union, intimate, exclusive and indissoluble, with the divine bridegroom, who has given himself to humanity without reserve and forever, thus acquiring a holy people, the Church. Inscribed in the human creature as a capacity to live in communion within the difference between man and woman, for consecrated virginity the spousal experience is one of transcendence and the surprising humility of God. Consecration takes place through the pact of covenant and fidelity that unites the virgin to the Lord in a mystical marriage, deepening and enlarging her sharing in his mind and her conformation to his desire to love.

25. The spousal union thus reveals its generative capacity, manifesting the abundance of divine grace[33]. In imitation of the

[33] «Spousal love always involves a special readiness to be poured out for the sake of those who come within one's

Church, whose daughters they are, consecrated virgins open themselves to the gift of spiritual maternity, becoming co-operators with the Spirit. Spiritual maternity is the gift of fruitful and hospitable interiority, that in relationships with others is a caring and courageous guardian of human dignity. It is an educative wisdom that seeks to offer favourable conditions for an encounter with God, and introduces and accompanies the journey along the paths of the Spirit.

26. The most splendid and harmonious integration of virginity, marriage and maternity is realized in the person of the Virgin Mary[34], the first fruits of humanity renewed in Christ. She is the perfect icon of the Church as mystery of communion, the woman in whom is already fulfilled the destiny of glory to which all humanity is called, and « mother of the living Gospel »[35]. In the *Kecharitoméne*

range of activity. In marriage this readiness, even though open to all, consists mainly in the love that parents give to their children. In virginity this readiness is open *to all people, who are embraced by the love of Christ the Spouse*»: John Paul II, Apostolic Letter *Mulieris dignitatem* (15 August 1988), 21.

[34] Second Vatican Ecumenical Council, Dogmatic Constitution on the Church *Lumen gentium*, VIII.

[35] Francis, Apostolic Exhortation *Evangelii gaudium* (24 November 2013), 287.

– *she who is has been filled with grace* (*Lk* 1:28) – the Church has always recognised the *Virgo virginum* (Virgin of virgins), the unsurpassable prototype of consecrated virginity[36]. Thus Mary is the mother, sister and teacher of consecrated virgins. In her, consecrated women find the model of attitudes of the heart: in listening to and welcoming the Word of God (*Lk* 8:21); in an active search for his will; in advancing on her pilgrimage of faith (*Jn* 2:1-5)[37], « towards a destiny of service and fruitfulness »[38]; in her total, free availability to carry out God's plan, « the contemplative of the mystery of God in our world, in human history and in the daily lives »[39] of one and all; in her virginal maternity (*Lk* 1:38); in her capacity to be « the woman of prayer and work in Nazareth, [...] our Lady of alacrity, who sets out from her town "without delay" (*Lk* 1:39) »[40]; in standing at the foot of the cross, hoping against hope (*Jn* 19:25), and in her care of the infant Church (*Acts* 1:14).

[36] Cf. Ambrosius, *De virginibus*, lib. II, c. 3, n. 19: *PL* 16, 211.

[37] Cf. John Paul II, Encyclical letter *Redemptoris Mater* (25 March 1987), 6.

[38] Francis, Apostolic Exhortation *Evangelii gaudium* (24 November 2013), 287.

[39] *Ivi*, 288.

[40] *Ibid.*

The form of life

Following the Gospel and personal charisms

27. Consecrated women find in the Gospel an inexhaustible source of the joy that gives meaning to their life, direction to their path and their fundamental rule[41]. Setting out to follow Christ, they embrace his chaste, poor and obedient way of life[42], and dedicate themselves to prayer, penance, the works of mercy and the apostolate, each one according to her own charisms[43].

In the *Ordo virginum* the vocation to virginity is harmonised with the charisms that give a concrete form to the witness and ecclesial service of each consecrated woman[44].

[41] Cf. Francis, Apostolic Exhortation *Evangelii gaudium* (24 November 2013), 1.

[42] Cf. Benedict XVI, *Speech to the participants at the Congress of the Ordo virginum on the theme: "Consecrated virginity in the world: a gift for the Church and in the Church"*, Rome (15 May 2008), 5; John Paul II, Post-synodal Apostolic Exhortation *Vita consecrata* (25 March 1996), 18.

[43] Cf. *Ordo consecrationis virginum, Prænotanda,* 2.

[44] «The charismatic gifts [...] are freely distributed by the Holy Spirit, so that sacramental grace may be fruitful in Christian life in different ways and at every level. Because these charisms "are perfectly suited to and useful for the needs of the Church", through their diverse richness, the People of God are able fully to live their evangelical mission, discerning the signs of the times and interpreting them in the light of the Gospel. The charismatic

These gifts – differing sensibilities, spiritual intuitions, plans and lifestyles – are thus brought to maturity within her, as an expression of her total and full dedication to the Lord[45].

28. So that personal charisms can be recognised, accepted and lived in their authenticity, consecrated women let themselves be accompanied and supported by the Church in the ongoing exercise of humble discernment, in order to understand what the will of God might be for their lives (*Rm* 12:2). This involves interpreting intelligently and with evangelical wisdom the spiritual experience of each consecrated woman, keeping in mind her life history and situating her in the

gifts, in fact, enable the faithful to respond to the gift of salvation in complete freedom and in a way suited to the times. In this way, they themselves become a gift of love for others and authentic witnesses to the Gospel before all mankind»: CONGREGATION FOR THE DOCTRINE OF THE FAITH, Letter *Iuvenescit Ecclesia* (15 May 2016), 15.

[45] «There are among you different approaches and different ways of living the gift of consecrated virginity [...]. I urge you to go beyond external appearances, experiencing the mystery of God's tenderness which each one of you bears in herself and recognizing one another as sisters, even in your diversity»: BENEDICT XVI, *Speech to the participants at the Congress of the* Ordo virginum *on the theme: «Consecrated virginity in the world: a gift for the Church and in the Church»*, Rome (15 May 2008), 5.

concrete ecclesial and social context in which she lives.

From among the assistance the Church recommends for discernment, consecrated women should not overlook spiritual accompaniment[46]. Sincere, responsive adult dialogue with a prudent, experienced person who practices this ministry, offers each one valuable opportunities to deepen, review, confirm and to suggest suitable means for growth in her response to the Lord who calls her to holiness and to personal integration.

In continuity with the path of vocational discernment leading to admission to consecration, in an attitude of filial obedience consecrated women consult the diocesan Bishop for guidance about more important aspects of their plan of life, and they confirm their decisions with him[47].

[46] «Confident and humble recourse to *spiritual direction* is of great help on the path of fidelity to the Gospel, especially in the period of formation and at certain other times in life. Through it individuals are helped to respond with generosity to the movement of the Spirit, and to direct themselves resolutely towards holiness»: John Paul II, Post-synodal Apostolic Exhortation *Vita consecrata* (25 March 1996), 95.

[47] Benedict XVI, *Speech to the participants at the Congress of the* Ordo virginum *on the theme: «Consecrated virginity in the world: a gift for the Church and in the Church»*, Rome (15 May 2008), 4-5.

Prayer and the ascetic path

29. For consecrated women, prayer is a necessity of love, to «contemplate the beauty of the one who loves them»[48], and of communion with the Beloved and with the world in which they are inserted.

Therefore, they love contemplative silence[49], which creates favourable conditions for listening to the Word of God and for heart-to-heart conversation with the Bridegroom. Desiring to deepen their understanding of him and the dialogue of prayer, they acquire familiarity with biblical revelation, above all through *lectio divina* and in-depth study of the scriptures[50].

30. In the liturgy they recognise the fountain of theological life and of ecclesial communion and mission. They allow their spirituality to be shaped by the celebration of the sacraments and the Liturgy of the Hours, in

[48] AUGUSTINUS, *De sancta virginitate*, c. 54: *PL* 40, 428.

[49] «The great patristic tradition teaches us that the mysteries of Christ all involve silence. Only in silence can the Word of God find a home in us, as it did in Mary»: BENEDICT XVI, Post-synodal Apostolic Exhortation *Verbum Domini* (30 September 2010), 66.

[50] «Ignorance of the Scriptures is ignorance of Christ»: HIERONYMUS, *Commentarii in Isaiam, Prologus*; *CCL* 73, 1: *PL* 24, 17.

obedience to the rhythm of the liturgical year. In this way, other practices of prayer, the ascetic path and their whole existence will find unity and direction.

31. For consecrated virgins, the liturgical year is the "educative path" travelled together with others towards an encounter with Christ the Bridegroom. They have confidence, therefore, in the Church's teaching to guide their deeper understanding, celebration and assimilation of the mysteries of Christ.

32. They place the Eucharist at the centre of their existence. It is the sacrament of the spousal covenant from which flows the grace of their consecration[51]. Called to live in intimacy with the Lord, identifying with him and conforming to him, sharing in the celebration of the Eucharist where possible every day, they receive the Bread of life from the table of the Word of God and the Body of Christ[52].

[51] « [The Eucharist] is the Sacrament of the Bridegroom and the Bride. The Eucharist makes present and realizes anew in a sacramental manner the redemptive act of Christ, who "creates" the Church, his body. Christ is united with this "body" as the bridegroom with the bride »: JOHN PAUL II, Apostolic letter *Mulieris dignitatem* (15 August 1988), 26.

[52] « Here the fullness of intimacy with Christ is realized, becoming one with him, total conformity to him to whom consecrated persons are called by vocation »: CONGREGATION FOR INSTITUTES OF CONSECRATED LIFE AND SOCIETIES OF APOS-

They express the love of the Church as Bride for the Eucharist also in the prayer of adoration of the Eucharistic Body of the Lord, and from him they draw effective charity towards the members of his mystical Body.

33. The frequent celebration of the sacrament of reconciliation «will allow [them] to touch the grandeur of God's mercy with their own hands». It is the «wellspring of true interior peace»[53]. that leads them back to the one Love of their life. Turning to the ministry of the Church with confidence, celebrating and praising God's prevenient and healing love, they recognise their own faults, renew their profession of faith in his mercy and relish the joy of forgiveness, which gives new energy for the path of conversion and fidelity to the Lord[54].

34. With daily fidelity to the Divine Office, which they received as a gift and have taken on as a duty in the rite of consecration,

TOLIC LIFE, Instruction *Starting afresh from Christ. A renewed commitment to consecrated life in the third millennium* (19 May 2002), 26.

[53] FRANCIS, Bull *Misericordiae vultus* (11 April 2015), 17.

[54] «To celebrate the sacrament of reconciliation means to be wrapped in a warm embrace, the embrace of the infinite mercy of the Father»: FRANCIS, *Audience* (19 February 2014).

they extend through time the memory of salvation and allow the extraordinary abundance of the paschal mystery to flow and spread through every hour of their life. Celebrating the Liturgy of the Hours, in particular Morning and Evening Prayer[55], they let the sentiments of Christ echo through them, absorbing them. They unite their voices to those of the entire Church, presenting to the Father the often unconscious cries of joy and sorrow that rise from humanity and from the whole of creation.

35. To deepen and rekindle their relationship with the Lord Jesus, they reserve appropriate times for retreats and the spiritual exercises. They take advantage of forms and methods of prayer that belong to the Church's tradition, including pious practices and other expressions of popular piety.

They cultivate a devotion to the Virgin Mary that is full of affection and filial trust. She is the «teacher of virginity»[56], model and patron of every consecrated life[57], from whom they daily learn to glorify the Lord.

36. Moved by a desire to respond to the Bridegroom's love with a love that grows in

[55] Cf. *Ordo consecrationis virginum, Prænotanda*, 2.

[56] AMBROSIUS, *De institutione virginis*, c. 6, n. 46: *PL* 16, 320.

[57] Cf. *Code of Cannon Law*, can. 663 § 4.

purity and generosity, they draw from prayer the inspiration for their choices. They exercise constant vigilance over their own behaviour and attitudes, accepting peacefully the sacrifices that daily life imposes on them. They struggle against temptations, thoughts, suggestions and options that lead to evil. They learn to receive the assistance of fraternal correction with humility.

They accept the penitential practices proposed by the Church and, in agreement with her spiritual director, each one chooses the ascetical forms or practices[58] that help her to grow in freedom and the evangelical virtues, with a disposition of discernment and conversion[59] that lasts through life[60].

[58] «Asceticism, by helping to master and correct the inclinations of human nature wounded by sin, is truly indispensable if consecrated persons are to remain faithful to their own vocation and follow Jesus on the way of the Cross»: John Paul II, Post-synodal Apostolic Exhortation *Vita consecrata* (25 March 1996), 38.

[59] «The vocation of consecrated persons to seek first the Kingdom of God is first and foremost a call to complete conversion, in self-renunciation, in order to live fully for the Lord, so that God may be all in all. Called to contemplate and bear witness to the transfigured face of Christ, consecrated men and women are also called to a transfigured existence»: John Paul II, Post-synodal Apostolic Exhortation *Vita consecrata* (25 March 1996), 35.

[60] «This then, is the rule of conversion: to distance yourself from evil and to learn to do good. Converting oneself

Styles of life, personal relationships and service

37. A characteristic of this form of life is the insertion of consecrated women in the particular Church, and thus in a specific cultural and social context. Consecration reserves them to God without distancing them from the environment in which they live and in which they are called to give personal witness[61].

They can live alone, with their family, together with other consecrated women or in other situations that facilitate the expression of their vocation and the fulfilment of their plan of life. They support themselves from the proceeds of their own work and their personal resources.

38. Desirous of irradiating the dignity and beauty of their vocation with a relational style towards the people of their own time, their way of dressing follows the local customs, combining dignity and the expression

is a journey. It is a journey which requires courage, to remove yourself from evil and humility to learn to do good. And above all, it requires concrete acts»: FRANCIS, Morning meditation in the Chapel of *Domus Sanctae Marthae, Learn to do good* (14 March 2017).

[61] Cf. BENEDICT XVI, *Speech to the participants at the Congress of the* Ordo virginum *on the theme: «Consecrated virginity in the world: a gift for the Church and in the Church»*, Rome (15 May 2008), 4-5.

of their own personality with the virtue of moderation, in accordance with the requirements of their social situation[62].

Except for special reasons, they wear the ring that is given to them during the rite of consecration as a sign of their spousal covenant with Christ the Lord.

In places where married Christian women do not customarily cover their head with a veil, normally consecrated virgins do not wear the veil that they may have received during the rite of consecration as an ordinary part of their clothing. They follow the guidelines of the diocesan Bishop or the Episcopal Conference, who can allow the use of the veil in liturgical celebrations, or in other situations where the use of this visible sign of total dedication to the service of Christ and the Church is considered appropriate, considering different contexts and developments in socio-cultural conditions.

39. Their dedication to the Church is shown in their «mission of illumining, blessing, enlivening, raising up, healing, and freeing»[63], in their passion for proclaiming the

[62] Francis, Encyclical Letter *Laudato si'* (24 May 2015), 222-227.

[63] Francis, Apostolic Exhortation *Evangelii gaudium* (24 November 2013), 273.

Gospel, for building up the Christian community and for their prophetic witness of fraternal communion, in friendship offered to all, in caring proximity to the spiritual and material needs of the people of their time, in the commitment to work for the common good of society[64].

This leads them to discern the concrete forms of their ecclesial service, which can also be expressed in their availability for pastoral ministries and appointments.

In accord with this, so that the knowledge of the mystery of Christ facilitates understanding the ministers of the Church, it is important that they reach maturity, through prayer and meditation as well as through concrete experience, in a profound and correct ministerial awareness, respectful of the mysterious evangelical and ecclesial wisdom that is also expressed in the dispositions of the Diocesan Bishops and of the Episcopal

[64] «To be authentic evangelizers, we need to develop a spiritual taste for being close to people's lives and to discover that this is itself a source of spiritual joy. Mission is at once a passion for Jesus and a passion for his people. […] He wants to make use of us to draw closer to his beloved people. He takes us from the midst of his people and he sends us to his people; without this sense of belonging we cannot understand our deepest identity»: FRANCIS, Apostolic Exhortation *Evangelii gaudium* (24 November 2013), 268.

Conferences. Educating themselves at the school of this wisdom, they will learn to receive, also through experience, both the suggestions that emerge from the life of the Church, which is the mystery of communion, and «all the hidden evangelical possibilities, that are already present and operative in the realities of the world»[65], so as to recognize the new opportunities that form a new ministerial consciousness, corresponding to the effective capacity of their generous gift of self.

Alert to the calls that come from the context in which they live and ready to put at the disposition of the Lord the gifts they have received from Him, they are called to make their own contribution to the renewal of society in the spirit of the Gospel. They accept without naivety or oversimplification the responsibility to develop cultural expressions of the faith and they adopt as their own the Church's preference for those who are poor, suffering or marginalised[66].

[65] Paolo VI, Apostolic Exhortation *Evangelii nuntiandi* (8 December 1975), 70.

[66] Cf. *Ordo consecrationis virginum*, 16; John Paul II, *Speech to the participants in the International Conference of the* Ordo virginum *on the 25th anniversary of the promulgation of the rite*, Rome (2 June 1995), n. 6; Francis, Apostolic Exhortation, *Evangelii gaudium* (24 November 2013), 197-216. «For the

40. Conscious of these responsibilities, they choose occupations in accordance with their own abilities, inclinations and opportunities. They recognise these as a practical way of giving witness that God calls humanity to collaboration in his work of creation and redemption, to share more intimately in the love with which he draws the world and its entire history to himself.

In the satisfaction and struggles that work entails, consecrated women develop their capacity to contemplate and promote the deepest and most fundamental meaning of human activity: to contribute to making the world a hospitable home for everyone, open to welcoming the manifestation of the Kingdom of God. Thus, they commit themselves in the sphere of work to achieving that « multiform personal development » that includes « creativity, future plans, the development of one's capacities, the exercise of values, communication with others, and a disposition of adoration »[67]. They take care to acquire and update their professional competence, and

Church, the option for the poor is primarily a theological category rather than a cultural, sociological, political or philosophical one »: Francis, Apostolic Exhortation, *Evangelii gaudium* (24 November 2013), 198.

[67] Francis, Encyclical Letter *Laudato si'* (24 May 2015), 127.

to oppose everything that degrades and obscures the dignity of human work.

41. They develop a sense of gratitude for God's work[68], contemplation filled with praise, a taste for beauty, a sensitivity to both festivity and relaxation[69], attention to every dimension of the person.

They learn from the Bridegroom, meek and humble of heart (*Mt* 11:29), to live in hope and to abandon to God their advancing age, with its successive phases of life, illness, moral suffering and other situations in which they experience the drama, fragility and uncertainty of existence[70].

Right to the end they embrace the spousal love of the Crucified and Risen one, entrusting themselves to Him, expressing even in death the paschal meaning of existence.

Through their personal consecration they remind everyone that the origin, the direction and the goal of human history is found in the holy mystery of God, in his infinite prevenient and merciful goodness and in the love that he wants to share with all creatures.

[68] *Ibid.*, 220.

[69] *Ibid.*, 237.

[70] Cf. John Paul II, *Speech to the participants in the International Conference of the* Ordo virginum *on the 25th anniversary of the promulgation of the rite*, Rome (2 June 1995), 4.

II.

THE CONFIGURATION OF THE *ORDO VIRGINUM* IN THE PARTICULAR CHURCHES AND IN THE UNIVERSAL CHURCH

Insertion in the Diocese

42. The women who receive this consecration are called to let charity shine through their lives, charity that is the principle of unity and holiness in the whole body of the Church. They remain inserted in that part of the people of God in which they already live and in the heart of which their vocational discernment and the preparation for their consecration is carried out. They are, in fact, bound by a special bond of love and mutual belonging to this particular Church.

The particular Church, in its diverse parts, is called to welcome the vocation of consecrated women, and to accompany and support their journey, recognising that virginal consecration and the personal charisms of each consecrated woman are gifts for the building up of the community and the ecclesial mission.

43. Consecrated women cultivate a sense of gratitude for all the gifts that they have received within the communion of saints, and that they continue to receive through the life of the particular Church in which they live: faith in the Lord Jesus, virginal consecration, a share in the history of sanctity incarnate in a spiritual tradition, developed in relation to the culture and institutions of a specific human community living in a certain place.

They pay constant attention to the magisterium of the diocesan Bishop and they respond to his pastoral decisions, accepting them responsibly, with intelligence and creativity.

They bring to prayer the needs of the Diocese and, in particular, the intentions of the Bishop.

They acknowledge as gifts of the Spirit the testimony of the other vocations that enrich the life of the Christian community and they benefit from opportunities for mutual edification and of pastoral, missionary, and charitable cooperation[71].

[71] Cf. *Code of Canon Law,* can. 680.

With their own feminine sensitivity[72], they offer their experience and reflection as a valuable contribution to the evangelical discernment that the Christian community is called to engage in at all times, regarding its manner of presence and action in the specific social context.

Communion and co-responsibility in the diocesan *Ordo virginum*

44. Belonging to the *Ordo virginum* implies a strong bond of communion between all the consecrated women present in the Diocese. They acknowledge each other as beloved sisters, with whom they share the same consecration and a burning passion for the Church's development. Thus, they welcome the spirit of communion as a gift and commit themselves to foster its growth, cultivating mutual respect, appreciating each one's gifts, nurturing friendship and raising awareness of particular cases of need (*Rm* 12:10,13,15-16). They maintain a close bond with their deceased sisters through prayer, treasuring the memory of their witness of love and fidelity to the Lord.

[72] Francis, Apostolic Exhortation *Evangelii gaudium* (24 November 2013), 103-104.

45. Consecrated women take an active part in formation initiatives, in agreement with the Bishop. They collaborate as far as possible in the formation of aspirants and candidates for consecration.

Considering the number of consecrated women and the practical circumstances, together with the diocesan Bishop they identify ways to provide a service of communion that fosters mutual understanding and stable relationships between them, promotes the exercise of co-responsibility in a synodal manner[73] and gives continuity and integration to common initiatives, without establishing relationships of hierarchical subordination between the consecrated women.

As an expression of the service of communion, a service or team can be established for vocational discernment and formation prior to consecration, and a service or team for permanent formation.

[73] «It is precisely this path of *synodality* which God expects of the Church of the third millennium»: FRANCIS, *Address on the occasion of the commemoration of the 50th Anniversary of the institution of the Synod of Bishops*, Rome (17 October 2015).

The responsibilities of the diocesan Bishop

46. The diocesan Bishop has the duty to welcome vocations to consecration in the *Ordo virginum* as a gift of the Spirit. He is to foster conditions so that the insertion of consecrated women in the Church entrusted to him will contribute to the path of holiness and the mission of the people of God.

In continuity with the ancient ecclesial tradition, the *Ordo consecrationis virginum* outlines the role of the diocesan Bishop, not only in his task as priestly dispenser of divine grace[74], but also as teacher who points out and confirms the path of faith[75], and as pastor who lovingly cares for the people entrusted to him[76].

His pastoral concern towards the *Ordo virginum* is in fact a part of the ordinary ministry of sanctification, teaching and governing of the diocesan Bishop. He has this obligation with respect to each individual consecrated woman, to women who aspire to receive consecration and also to the *Ordo virginum* of his Diocese as a group.

[74] Cf. *Ordo consecrationis virginum, Prænotanda*, 6.

[75] Cf. *Ordo consecrationis virginum*, 14 and 16.

[76] Cf. *Ordo consecrationis virginum, Prænotanda*, 5; *Ordo consecrationis virginum*, 2 and 16.

47. As the one responsible for admission to consecration, the diocesan Bishop oversees the collection of information about each candidate, establishes the ways in which a suitable course of formation is carried out and finalizes the vocational discernment.

With the celebration of consecration, the Bishop presents the consecrated women to the ecclesial community as a sign of the Church as the Bride of Christ. Since the ordinary minister of consecration is the diocesan Bishop[77], it will not be possible to celebrate it when the see is vacant (*sede vacante*). Only in case of true necessity will the diocesan Bishop resort to the delegation of the faculty to celebrate it. Through the celebration of the rite, even if it is carried out for a single person, the *Ordo virginum* is rendered present in the particular Church, without the necessity of another act of establishment by the Bishop.

48. The diocesan Bishop exercises pastoral care of the consecrated women, encouraging them to live in joyful fidelity to their own vocation. He is attentive to the needs of each one's progress and ensures the availability of suitable means of ongoing formation.

[77] Cf. *Ordo consecrationis virginum, Prænotanda*, 6.

He supports communion among the consecrated women and the sense of co-responsibility for the vitality of their ecclesial witness. He promotes opportunities for gatherings, activities and common formation programs. At the diocesan level, in agreement with the consecrated women, he arranges ways in which the service of communion can be planned, taking into account the particular circumstances. He also encourages contacts and collaboration with consecrated women in other Dioceses.

49. Taking his part, together with the other consecrated women, he is attentive towards consecrated women who are going through times of serious suffering or hardships due to advanced age, poor health or other difficult situations.

Keeping local customs and circumstances in mind, he provides guidelines for the consecrated women to ensure prayers of suffrage for the deceased women, safeguarding the memory of their witness of faith and love of the Lord. As far as possible, they make themselves available to participate in the celebration of Christian funeral services for these sisters and share the preparation with relatives and other persons close to them.

50. Even if a Delegate has been named for the pastoral care of the *Ordo virginum*, the final decision concerning acts of major importance remains the competence of the diocesan Bishop. Such acts include: admission to consecration; inscription of a consecrated woman from another Diocese into the diocesan *Ordo virginum*; dispensation from the obligations of consecration; dismissal from the *Ordo virginum*; provision of directives for the formation prior to consecration and for permanent formation; approval of programs for carrying out the service of communion of the diocesan *Ordo virginum*; the establishment of canonical foundations to provide support and financial management for the activities of the *Ordo virginum* and possible authorization to request their civil recognition; recognition and approval of the statutes of the diocesan association of consecrated virgins, as well as possible authorization to request their civil recognition.

51. The Bishop will give the necessary instructions for the inscription of women to be consecrated in a suitable book to be safeguarded in the diocesan curia, and for the careful collection of documentation concerning the *Ordo virginum*. In particular, the following must be recorded: the deaths of consecrated women; the ascription or temporary acceptance into the diocesan *Ordo virginum* of consecrated women from other Dioceses; the temporary or definitive transfer of consecrated women to other Dioceses; transfer to an Institute of consecrated life; the granting of dispensations from the obligations of consecration; and dismissal from the *Ordo virginum*. Documentation will also be kept about the formative program of each separate aspirant and candidate for consecration.

Collaboration in the pastoral care of the *Ordo virginum*

52. Bearing in mind the concrete circumstances, the diocesan Bishop will decide what assistance is needed to ensure appropriate pastoral care[78] for the *Ordo virginum*, in keeping with the special characteristics of this form of life.

He can appoint a Delegate, preferably chosen either from the diocesan presbyterate or from the consecrated virgins of the Diocese, for the pastoral care of the *Ordo vir-*

[78] Cf. CONGREGATION FOR BISHOPS, Directory for the Pastoral Ministry of Bishops *Apostolorum Successores* (22 February 2004), 104.

ginum, defining the scope of the appointment and its specific duties, and specifying how he/she should relate with the episcopal Vicar for consecrated life, where present.

If a service of communion is established, the Bishop will decide how the activities of the Delegate must be integrated with it in its various expressions, in particular with the teams for formation prior to consecration and permanent formation.

53. Following the guidelines given by the Bishop, pastoral collaboration may involve knowledge of each aspirant and candidate with a view to gathering the necessary information for discernment for admission to consecration, as well as the promotion of formation prior to consecration and permanent formation, either by helping to draw up personal formation programs, or by suggesting shared formative experiences.

Regarding pastoral collaboration in the external forum, those entrusted with these responsibilities will not establish a spiritual accompaniment relationship with aspirants, candidates or consecrated women. They know that their personal dialogue with each one is to be used specifically for listening, challenge and review of progress. They can also invite the person to approach the diocesan Bishop when direction or review about more important aspects of her life plan might be useful.

54. The aim of the pastoral care of the *Ordo virginum* is to help each aspirant, candidate and consecrated woman to develop the gifts she has received from the Lord; to promote communion among all the women and a sense of co-responsibility in accepting legitimate differences; to foster intelligent and responsible acceptance of the magisterium and the pastoral decisions of the diocesan Bishop; and to promote awareness of the *Ordo virginum* among the people of God.

Communion and co-responsibility between consecrated women of different Dioceses

55. In their relationships with consecrated women in other Dioceses, consecrated women welcome and cultivate the gift of communion and the commitment to the mission that arises from having received the same consecration.

Diocesan insertion in fact, is in harmony with the sense of belonging to an *ordo fidelium* with the same essential characteristics in the whole Catholic Church.

Through prayer for one another, reciprocal knowledge and the sharing of experiences and formative activities, consecrated women express in a variety of ways their co-responsibility for the witness they are called to give in the Church and in the world.

Shared activities, the service of communion and the Bishops' representative

56. Within groupings of particular Churches, in agreement with the Bishops of the respective Episcopal conferences, consecrated women can organise shared initiatives and, if the circumstances allow, a permanent service of communion. This can facilitate the interchange of their experiences of living in the Dioceses to which they belong, the development of topics of common interest, the proposal of content and methods suitable for formation programs at every stage, the presentation to the Bishops of useful suggestions and recommendations to help define the presence of the *Ordo virginum* in the different ecclesial and socio-cultural contexts, and promote awareness of the *Ordo virginum* among the people of God.

Shared initiatives and the service of communion must always respect and enhance the diocesan basis of this form of life and involve the consecrated women of the Dioceses concerned in a synodal style of participation.

57. The Bishops gathered in an Episcopal conference can draw up common guidelines for their Dioceses for the pastoral care of the *Ordo virginum.* They can also entrust to one Bishop the task of being their representative for the *Ordo virginum.*

While respecting the irreplaceable role of the diocesan Bishops in the pastoral care of consecrated virgins in their own Dioceses, the Bishops' representative expresses the interest of his fellow Bishops in this form of consecrated life, and their concern for and closeness to it.

Having at heart that the specific identity of the *Ordo virginum* be adequately expressed in the ecclesial and socio-cultural context of the Dioceses involved, the Bishops' representative carries out his duties to serve the effective exercise of co-responsibility on the part of the consecrated women of the different Dioceses. He attentively follows the shared activities of the consecrated women of the Dioceses involved, and where it has been established, he lends the assistance of his ministry to their permanent service of communion.

Reference to the Apostolic See and the Secretariat for the Ordo virginum

58. The consecrated women acknowledge the ministry of the Successor of Peter as the focal point towards which they converge to live at the level of the universal Church, in living the gift of communion and the co-responsibility of belonging to the same *ordo fidelium.*

In synergy with the magisterium and action of the diocesan bishops and in accordance with their own competence, the Congregation for Institutes of Consecrated Life and Societies of Apostolic Life is at the service of the growth of the *Ordo virginum,* so that this form of consecrated life might be recognized, valued, and promoted in its specific identity and ecclesial configuration.

59. A secretariat for the *Ordo virginum* is established in the Dicastery. Under the direction of the Prefect, the Secretariat collects the data about the situation of the *Ordo virginum* in the various countries. It also notes the comments included by the Bishops in the reports presented on their *ad limina* visits.

In addition, it is the reference point for initiatives concerning the *Ordo virginum* that are promoted or supported by the Diocese itself.

To assist its work, the Secretariat can avail itself of the help of consecrated women from various places, the Episcopal Conferences and the Bishops' representatives for the *Ordo virginum* where these have been appointed.

Residence in another Diocese and transfer

60. Although consecration establishes a special insertion in the particular Church in which it is celebrated, it does not prevent consecrated women from transferring to another particular Church, if necessary, either permanently or on a temporary basis, for example for employment, family or pastoral purposes or for other reasonable and proportionate motives.

61. When a consecrated woman intends to remain for a long period in a Diocese different from the one to which she belongs, with the agreement of her own Bishop she can ask the Bishop of the Diocese *ad quem* (to whom) if she can participate in the formation activities of the local *Ordo virginum*. When she has been introduced by her own diocesan Bishop to the Bishop of the Diocese *ad quem* (from which), the latter will arrange with her the manner of her participation.

62. If a consecrated woman intends to transfer permanently to another Diocese, she will explain her reasons to her own Bishop, who will give her his opinion on the proposal. She can then ask the Bishop of the Diocese *ad quem* for acceptance into the local *Ordo virginum.* The latter, having received an introduction of the consecrated woman from the Bishop of the Diocese *a quo,* giving the reasons for the transfer and his own opinion, will make his decision and communicate his response to the applicant. He will also inform the Bishop of the Diocese *a quo.* If the response is positive, the Bishop of the Diocese *ad quem* will accept the consecrated woman, present her to his particular Church, and if there are consecrated women in his Diocese, he will include her among them. He will arrange with her what will be necessary and useful for her personal situation. Based on an evaluation, the Bishop of the Diocese *ad quem* can also refuse to accept her or, with the agreement of the Bishop of the Diocese *a quo,* can fix a time of probation. In this case, while maintaining her link with the Diocese *a quo,* the consecrated woman can nevertheless transfer her canonical domicile to the Diocese *ad quem*, abiding by the guidelines agreed with both Bishops concerning her personal situation.

63. Personally or through the Delegate, the Bishop will take care to inform the consecrated women in an appropriate way about the temporary or definitive transfer of a consecrated woman to another Diocese, and also about the acceptance of a consecrated woman from another Diocese.

Foundations, associations and the choice of communal living

64. Respecting the civil law, for the support and financial management of the activities of the *Ordo virginum* the diocesan Bishop can establish a canonical foundation, either non-autonomous or autonomous[79], and if needed, he can approve a request for its civil recognition.

65. To more faithfully fulfil their *propositum* and provide mutual assistance in carrying out the service to the Church in a way that befits their state, consecrated women can form associations and ask the competent ecclesial authority for canonical recognition

[79] Cf. *Code of Canon Law*, can. 1303 § 1.

of the statutes, and potentially, approval of the association[80].

The establishment of an association, or joining an association already established, is exclusively a free and voluntary choice for each one of the consecrated women who choose to accept its objectives and its statutes. The departure of a consecrated woman from the association does not negatively affect her belonging to the *Ordo virginum.*

66. The consecrated virgins who desire it can freely decide to live in the same house. This option, responsibly chosen for mutual assistance, for sharing life at the spiritual, pastoral or financial level, expresses the free decision of each of the consecrated virgins. It does not derive directly from consecration or from belonging to an association, unless its statutes prescribe common life as a constitutive element of the association itself.

Belonging to the *Ordo virginum* and involvement with other ecclesial groups

67. The form of life proper to the *Ordo virginum* is a particular path of sanctification with a characteristic spiritual identity that

[80] Cf. *Code of Canon Law,* can. 604 § 2.

unifies and directs the entire existence of the person. It is the task of each consecrated woman to offer a peaceful and joyful witness of her own consecration, so that she becomes an encouragement and a treasure for all parts of the Christian community.

This does not prevent a consecrated virgin from drawing on the variety of charisms and spiritualities with which the Spirit enriches the Church, and possibly finding help to express her own virginal charism in the context of a specific ecclesial group (Third Order, Association or Movement), its charism and its spirituality[81].

68. The authenticity of such a spiritual experience must be the object of discernment within spiritual accompaniment, and also in dialogue with the diocesan Bishop and the Delegate for the pastoral care of the *Ordo virginum*, if there is one, so that the interests of the group and involvement in its activities do not obscure the significance of diocesan insertion that is constitutive of the consecration lived in the *Ordo virginum*.

The consecrated woman shall take care to maintain an active experience of commun-

[81] Cf. Congregation for the Doctrine of the Faith, Letter *Iuvenescit Ecclesia* (15 May 2016), 16.

ion with the particular Church to which she belongs, through the necessary mediation of the diocesan Bishop, with filial acceptance of his teaching and his pastoral care. She shall also earnestly cultivate relationships of communion with the other consecrated virgins and will give priority to formative proposals specific to the *Ordo virginum* over any initiatives of the group with which she is involved.

Separation from the *Ordo virginum*

Transfer to an Institute of Consecrated Life or a Society of Apostolic Life

69. If a consecrated woman, after careful evaluation in prayer, in the context of spiritual direction and in dialogue with the Bishop, wishes to enter an Institute of consecrated life or Society of Apostolic Life, she will communicate her intention in writing to the Bishop, accompanied by a declaration from the Supreme Moderator of the Institute concerning the contact that the consecrated woman has had with that Institute or Society[82].

The Bishop will undertake to transmit the request to the Holy See and his possible ob-

[82] Cf. *Code of Canon Law,* cann. 684 and 685.

servations on the matter. Transfer to the Institute will take place according to the arrangements made for each particular case by the Holy See.

Departure from the Ordo virginum

70. If a consecrated woman, for very serious reasons evaluated before the Lord in careful discernment, wishes to be dispensed from the obligations arising from consecration, she will approach her diocesan Bishop with a written request. The Bishop must not neglect to offer her appropriate assistance and adequate time for her discernment. He will grant the dispensation only after an in-depth scrutiny of the reasons for her request.

Dismissal from the Ordo virginum

71. If a consecrated woman has notoriously defected from the catholic faith or has contracted marriage, even only civilly, the Bishop will collect the evidence and declare her dismissal from the *Ordo virginum*, so that it is recognised juridically.

72. If a consecrated woman is accused of very serious[83] external and imputable

[83] Cf. *Code of Canon Law*, can. 695.

crimes or failings against the obligations arising from her consecration, such as to cause scandal among the people of God, the Bishop will begin the process of dismissal. He will therefore inform the woman about the accusations and the proofs that have been collected, giving her the opportunity for defence.

If the Bishop considers her defence insufficient, and there is no other way to provide for her correction, for the restoration of justice and reparation of the scandal, he will dismiss her from the *Ordo virginum*. The decree of dismissal must express at least in summary form the reasons for the decision. It will not take effect until it has been confirmed by the Holy See, to whom all the acts must be forwarded. The decree will not be valid if it does not indicate the consecrated woman's right to have recourse to the competent authority within ten days of receiving notification of the decree. The recourse has a suspensive effect.

Record-keeping and communication about separation

73. In all cases of the separation of a consecrated woman from the *Ordo virginum*, the diocesan Bishop will arrange for this to be recorded in the book of consecrations. He will take care to inform the other consecrated women about it, either personally or through the Delegate, and the Pastor responsible so that he may note it in the Baptismal register.

III.
VOCATIONAL DISCERNMENT AND FORMATION FOR THE *ORDO VIRGINUM*

Responsibility for discernment and formation

The faith journey, vocational discernment and formation programs

74. By virtue of faith, baptismal grace, the virginal charism and her own personal charisms, the woman who is called to consecration in the *Ordo virginum* is involved in a journey of Christian life, following the Lord Jesus. The dynamism of this path, generated by the Holy Spirit, requires her active response and her docile cooperation.

The following of the Lord consists in continual conversion, in a progressive fidelity to him[84]. It is a process that involves all the dimensions of existence, corporeal and affective, intellectual, volitional and spiritual.

[84] Cf. JOHN PAUL II, Post-Synodal Apostolic Exhortation *Vita consecrata* (25 March 1996), 19.

It extends throughout life, since the consecrated person « can never claim to have completely brought to life the new creature who, in every circumstance of life, reflects the very mind of Christ »[85].

75. The grace of consecration in the *Ordo virginum* defines and shapes the spiritual features of the person in a permanent way. It directs her on the path of life, and supports and strengthens her in an increasingly generous response to her call.

Consecration therefore not only requires growth in human and Christian maturity, evaluated through careful vocational discernment and specific prior formation. It also requires committed, constant attention to permanent formation that deepens and renews the reasons for the choice she has already made, and allows the consecrated woman to be strengthened in her own vocation at the same time that she is actually experiencing its intrinsic dynamism[86].

76. Given the insertion of this form of consecrated life in the particular Church, vocational discernment, formation prior to consecration and attention to permanent

[85] *Ibid.*, 69.

[86] *Ibid.*, 65 and 69-70.

formation take place through ecclesial programs that require the attention and accompaniment of the Christian community. They also demand responsibility on the part of the women themselves and in a particular way they call on the pastoral responsibility of the diocesan Bishop.

To gather the elements necessary for vocational discernment and to direct and accompany the programs of formation for the aspirants, candidates and the consecrated women, the Bishop can be assisted by the Delegate for the *Ordo virginum.* He will also make use of the contribution that the consecrated women are able to offer.

For this purpose, taking into account the number of consecrated women in the Diocese and their opinion on the matter and other practical considerations, the Bishop can also establish a service or team for vocational discernment and formation prior to consecration and a service or team for permanent formation, as expressions of the service of communion for the *Ordo virginum.* These services or teams shall consist of the Delegate, if the Bishop has appointed one, and consecrated women endowed with the necessary aptitudes, who are designated by the Bishop or the Delegate after consulting the consecrated women.

77. The formation plan will seek above all to draw out and strengthen the person's fundamental attitude of receptiveness, which includes freedom, the desire and the ability to learn from all situations of life, and taking an active and responsible part in the process of personal growth throughout the course of one's life[87].

For this reason, in drawing up the formation programs, attention is to be paid so that they are not reduced to standard or generic plans that do not take sufficient account of the specific needs and charisms of each person. At the same time vigilance is to be exercised about the risk of individualistic tendencies[88], which hinder the acquisition and

[87] «It will be important that all consecrated persons be formed in the freedom to learn throughout life, in every age and season, in every human ambient and context, from every person and every culture open to be taught by any fragment of truth and beauty found around them. But above all they must learn to be formed by everyday life, by their own community, by their brothers and sisters, by everyday things, ordinary and extraordinary, by prayer and by apostolic fatigue, in joy and in suffering, until the moment of death»: Congregation for Institutes of Consecrated Life and Societies of Apostolic Life, Instruction *Starting afresh from Christ. A renewed commitment to consecrated life in the third millennium* (19 May 2002), 15.

[88] « *This is the temptation of selfish people.* Along the way, they lose sight of the goal and, rather than think of others, they are unashamed to think only of themselves, or even

development of a true sense of ecclesial belonging and the spirit of communion within the *Ordo virginum*.

78. Since their purpose is to foster the development of the capacity to interpret reality according to evangelical criteria, formative programs must include, as indispensable elements: theological, cultural and pastoral formation, gradually increasing in depth and breadth, appropriate for the type of witness to which the consecrated women are called, acquired through personal study and formation meetings, possibly with experts; spiritual experiences, including personal and liturgical prayer, penitential practices, retreats and spiritual exercises that hold the person in an atmosphere of attentive listening and constant searching for the will of God; insertion in a network of ecclesial relationships to nurture the integral growth of the person and in particular to increase the potential of relationships between the aspirants and the consecrated women who contribute to the

worse, to justify themselves. The Church is the community of the faithful, the Body of Christ, where the salvation of one member is linked to the holiness of all. An individualist is a cause of scandal and of conflict»: FRANCIS, *Address on the occasion of the meeting and prayer with priests, religious and seminarians*, Cairo (29 April 2017).

formation service; spiritual accompaniment; and the sharing of experiences with and among the consecrated women.

Care will be taken to offer courses that are organically designed, with the progressive stages clearly defined and regularly reviewed. Attention to the formation of each aspirant, candidate and consecrated woman is accompanied by and integrated with joint programs for the whole group of aspirants, candidates and consecrated women.

The practice of spiritual accompaniment

79. Every phase of the process of discernment and formation requires the practice of spiritual accompaniment: a constant trusting relationship with a person who is gifted with a deep spirit of faith and Christian wisdom, whom each aspirant, candidate and consecrated woman can freely choose. This practice is a valuable aid not only for vocational discernment but also for decisions about the more important obligations in life.

To ensure the person's freedom in the area of manifestation of conscience, the Delegate for the pastoral care of the *Ordo virginum* and the consecrated women who participate in the service of formation offer this service in the external forum. They do not establish relationships of spiritual accompaniment with the aspirants, candidates or consecrated women. They abstain from asking for information or advice about the aspirants, candidates or consecrated women from their directors, spiritual accompaniers, and confessors.

Vocational discernment and the formation program prior to consecration

The dynamics of vocational discernment and formation prior to consecration

80. Vocational discernment consists in scrutinizing the signs by which the charism of the *Ordo virginum* is expressed, with its special insertion in the particular Church and its characteristic way of being present in the social and cultural context. For the good of the persons concerned and of the Church, it is necessary to foster conditions conducive to the operation of a peaceful and free discernment, in which to verify the authenticity of the vocation and the purity of motivation in the light of faith and of possible countersigns[89].

[89] Cf. Congregation for Institutes of Consecrated Life and Societies of Apostolic Life, Instruction *Starting afresh from Christ. A renewed commitment to consecrated life in the third millennium* (19 May 2002), 18.

The formation program prior to consecration must offer opportunities to verify the initial vocational insight. At the same time it must enkindle in the aspirants and candidates the desire for deeper union with the Lord Jesus, for a freer and more generous response to the Father's call, and for more attentive, intelligent and obedient conformity to the action of the Holy Spirit. One can only speak of a truly formative process if an authentic personal experience of conversion takes place, an experience of illumination, purification and deeper commitment to participation in the following of the Lord.

81. Vocational discernment ordinarily takes place in a process that includes an initial evaluation concerning admission to the formation process leading to consecration. It continues throughout this process and is completed when the diocesan Bishop makes a decision to admit to consecration. Three distinct opportunities can be distinguish for explanation and educational opportunities: the introductory or preparatory period; the period of formation appropriately divided into segments with their own objectives and evaluation; the period of final discernment or scrutiny.

82. In no case can the preparatory period begin before the age of eighteen years. For admission to consecration the usual age for marriage in the region must be taken into account[90]. Ordinarily consecration is not celebrated before the candidate has reached her twenty-fifth birthday.

83. It is the duty of the diocesan Bishop to specify the ways in which the programs of formation are to be implemented, in dialogue with the women involved and considering their individual circumstances and needs. Each one will be offered the possibility of deepening her knowledge of this form of life in its essential elements and of evaluating her own spiritual experience and her particular way of life in relation to these elements in a sincere and realistic way.

Care will be taken to maintain a close interconnection between vocational discernment and the formation program prior to consecration, because admission to the formation program does not imply an obligation for the candidate to ask for admission to consecration, nor an obligation for the Bishop to admit her to consecration.

[90] Cf. *Code of Canon Law*, can. 1072.

Prerequisites and criteria for discernment

84. Admission to consecration requires that the candidate gives evidence, with regard to her age, her human and spiritual maturity and the respect that she enjoys in the Christian community in which she is inserted, that she is able to assume the commitments that arise from consecration in a responsible manner[91].

It is also a prerequisite that the person has never been married and has never lived in public or open violation of chastity[92].

85. In vocational discernment, attention will be paid to the signs in the aspirant or candidate that give positive indications of her true vocation, including evidence of an intense and vivid spiritual experience, the authenticity of the motives that direct her towards consecration in the *Ordo virginum*, and the presence of the aptitudes necessary for perseverance in the life of consecration,

With pedagogical knowledge and in accordance with the principle of graduality, the presence of these signs will be ascer-

[91] Cf. *Ordo consecrationis virginum, Prænotanda,* 5 *b*).

[92] Cf. *Ordo consecrationis virginum, Prænotanda,* 5 *a*) and 5 *b*).

tained from the preparatory period, to make an assessment about admission to the formation program. They constitute essential reference points for the formation prior to consecration and the definitive discernment about admission to consecration.

86. In order to verify the spiritual experience, particular importance will be paid to:

a) her personal relationship with Christ and the desire to shape the whole of her being «to the Lord Jesus and to his *total self-giving*»[93] as a loving response to his infinite love[94];

b) the sense of belonging to the Church, experienced through sharing in the life of the Christian community, supported by a deep love for ecclesial communion, by the celebration of the sacraments and by an attitude of filial obedience to the diocesan Bishop;

c) attention to the contemplative dimension of her life and fidelity to spiritual discipline, to times, rhythms and various forms of prayer;

[93] John Paul II, Post-Synodal Apostolic Exhortation *Vita consecrata* (25 March 1996), 65.

[94] Cf. John Paul II, *Speech to the participants in the International Conference of the* Ordo virginum *on the 25th anniversary of the promulgation of the rite*, Rome (2 June 1995), 4.

d) diligence in penitential and ascetical practices and spiritual accompaniment;

e) eagerness to deepen her knowledge of scripture, the contents of the faith, liturgy, and the history and the magisterium of the Church;

f) passion for the Kingdom of God, which leads her to interpret the reality of her own times in accordance with evangelical criteria, and to respond to this reality with a sense of responsibility and a preferential love for those who are poor;

g) the presence of an comprehensive and global insight into her own vocation, which demonstrates a realistic understanding of her own history, her characteristics – her resources, limits, desires, aspirations and motivations – and which is consistent with the form of life of the *Ordo virginum*.

87. To confirm her human maturity, the following indications will be considered:

a) realistic self-knowledge and a calm, objective awareness of her own talents and limits, together with a clear capacity for self-determination and an appropriate attitude towards the assumption of responsibility;

b) the capacity to establish healthy, serene and generous relationships with men and women, together with a correct understanding of the value of marriage and motherhood;

c) the capacity to integrate her sexuality with her personal identity and to direct her affective energies in a way that expresses her own femininity through a chaste life that is open to a wider spiritual fruitfulness[95].

d) her professional skills and capacity to work so as to provide for her own sustenance in a dignified manner;

e) a proven aptitude to reframe suffering and frustration, and to give and receive for-

[95] «Benedict XVI spoke of an "ecology of man", based on the fact that "man too has a nature that he must respect and that he cannot manipulate at will" [*Address to the Deutscher Bundestag*, Berlin (22 September 2011)]. It is enough to recognize that our body itself establishes us in a direct relationship with the environment and with other living beings. The acceptance of our bodies as God's gift is vital for welcoming and accepting the entire world as a gift from the Father and our common home, whereas thinking that we enjoy absolute power over our own bodies turns, often subtly, into thinking that we enjoy absolute power over creation. Learning to accept our body, to care for it and to respect its fullest meaning, is an essential element of any genuine human ecology. Also, valuing one's own body in its femininity or masculinity is necessary if I am going to be able to recognize myself in an encounter with someone who is different. In this way we can joyfully accept the specific gifts of another man or woman, the work of God the Creator, and find mutual enrichment»: Francis, Encyclical Letter *Laudato si'* (24 May 2015), 155.

giveness, as possible steps towards the fullness of human nature;

f) fidelity to her word and to her commitments;

g) the responsible use of goods, of social media and of her free time.

88. In vocational guidance and when there is need to describe the characteristics of this vocation and the requirements for admission to consecration, the condition of virginity will be presented starting with the rich symbolism of its biblical foundations, within the framework of an anthropological vision solidly based on Christian revelation. On this basis the different dimensions, physical, psychological and spiritual, are integrated and considered in their dynamic connection to the lived history of the person and in openness to the unceasing action of divine grace that directs, guides and invigorates her on the path of holiness.

As a treasure of inestimable value that God pours into clay vessels (cf. *2 Cor* 4:7), this vocation is truly an undeserved gift. It encounters the person in her actual humanity, always in need of redemption and yearning for the full meaning of her existence. It finds its origin and dynamic centre in the grace of God, who unceasingly acts with the tenderness and the strength of his merciful love in the often complex and sometimes contradictory events of human life, helping the person to grasp her uniqueness and the unity of her being, enabling her to make a total gift of self. In this context it should be kept in mind that the call to give witness to the Church's virginal, spousal and fruitful love for Christ is not reducible to the symbol of physical integrity. Thus to have kept her body in perfect continence or to have practised the virtue of chastity in an exemplary way, while of great importance with regard to the discernment, are not essential prerequisites in the absence of which admittance to consecration is not possible.

The discernment therefore requires good judgement and insight, and it must be carried out individually. Each aspirant and candidate is called to examine her own vocation with regard to her own personal history, in honesty and authenticity before God, and with the help of spiritual accompaniment.

Recourse to expert psychologists

89. In vocational discernment and in the formation process prior to consecration, recourse to expert psychologists can be helpful in some cases[96]. If the vocation to consecrated virginity, as the fruit of a special gift of God, and its definitive discernment exceed the specific expertise of the psychologist, these elements can be integrated into the total context of discernment and formation, for a more reliable evaluation of the psychological status of the aspirant or candidate, her ability to respond to her vocation and for further assistance in her human growth.

A personality assessment can be prudently requested if doubts arise about the presence of a psychological disorder.

90. In every case, to be able to consult an expert psychologist, the free and informed prior written consent of the person concerned is necessary. Her good reputation and the right to defend her own personal privacy must always be protected[97].

In choosing experts to consult, not only must their professional competence be en-

[96] Cf. Congregation for Catholic Education, *Guidelines for the use of psychology in the admission and formation of candidates for the priesthood* (29 June 2008); Congregation for the Clergy, *The gift of the priestly vocation. Ratio Fundamentalis Institutionis Sacerdotalis* (8 December 2016), 146-147 and 191-196.

[97] Congregation for the Clergy, *The gift of the priestly vocation. Ratio Fundamentalis Institutionis Sacerdotalis* (8 December 2016), 194.

sured, but also whether they are inspired by an anthropology that openly shares the Christian understanding of the human person and the vocation to the consecrated life[98]. In addition, the professional confidentiality of the expert must always be respected.

91. If the evaluation reveals the presence of a psychological disorder or a serious problem, in vocational discernment the Bishop will take into account the nature of the disorder, its gravity and the way in which it influences the psyche of the person and therefore her aptitude for consecration.

The preparatory period

92. The goal of the preparatory period is to verify the qualifications and prerequisites necessary for a beneficial course of formation with a view to consecration.

The length of this course and the manner in which it takes place must allow an effective knowledge of the aspirant on the part of the Bishop, the Delegate and the consecrated women who participate in the service of for-

[98] «In the selection of specialists, other than their human qualities and competence in their field, their faith must also be taken into account»: CONGREGATION FOR THE CLERGY, *The gift of the priestly vocation. Ratio Fundamentalis Institutionis Sacerdotalis* (8 December 2016), 146.

mation, and at the same time allow the aspirant to acquire knowledge of the essential aspects of consecration and of the form of life proper to the *Ordo virginum*, in a way that helps her to relate them to her own vocational intuition. Ordinarily, one or two years duration should be given for this.

93. In dialogue with the Bishop, the Delegate or one of the consecrated women who participate in the service of formation, the aspirant will be invited to present her own story, her current life style and the reasons that led her towards this form of life.

At the beginning it is necessary to confirm that the aspirant has received the sacraments of Christian initiation and has never married, and to ascertain that she has never lived in public or open violation of chastity, that is, in a stable situation of cohabitation or in similar situations that would have been publicly known[99].

Taking into account her past faith journey and therefore the present situation and the preparation of each aspirant, programs of catechesis, study and reflection on consecrated life in general and on the fundamental aspects of Christian life can be offered.

[99] *Ordo consecrationis virginum, Prænotanda,* 5 *a*).

94. In regular meetings with the Bishop, the Delegate or one of the consecrated women who collaborate in the service of formation, the aspirant will be invited to review her own faith experience and her vocational understanding, beginning with some suggested themes.

In spiritual accompaniment, she will find further opportunities to reveal her past experiences, to re-examine the darker and more painful aspects of her life in the light of the Word of God, and to begin or to consolidate processes of interior healing that will enable her to be predisposed to accept the grace of her vocation more fully and freely.

Where possible, depending on the circumstances, the aspirant will be given opportunities to meet other consecrated women of the *Ordo virginum*, who can help the process of vocational discernment, also through their own testimony.

When there is a number of aspirants, it may be useful and convenient to arrange meetings where they can get to know each other and reflect together. Each aspirant, however, must have adequate opportunities for confidential personal dialogue with the Bishop, the Delegate or one of the consecrated women who collaborate in the service of formation.

95. Special attention must be paid to assessing the ways in which the aspirant participates in the life of the Christian community. This will enable knowledge about herself offered by the aspirant to be integrated appropriately with information from priests and other persons who know her well.

The aspirant can also be asked to present documentation about her studies and employment history.

To acquire the necessary elements for the evaluation of a person coming from another form of consecrated life, the Bishop will take care to collect the relevant information, including information from the Institute or Society concerned, in order to carry out a wise discernment. He will also require that the aspirant take adequate time to process her separation and will carefully ascertain how she is inserted in her ecclesial and social context.

96. At the end of the preparatory period, if the aspirant requests it, and the knowledge the Bishop has acquired about her leads him to believe that she can successfully proceed to the stage of formation prior to consecration, he will admit her to the formation program prior to consecration.

The formation program prior to consecration

97. The course of formation prior to consecration has the double objective of consolidating the Christian formation of the candidate and of offering her the necessary means to deepen her essential understanding of the characteristic elements and responsibilities that derive from consecration in the *Ordo virginum*.

The length of the program and the particular methods of implementation will facilitate an effective personal integration of the different elements of formation for each candidate, so that her decision to request admission to consecration can mature with sufficient awareness and freedom. Ordinarily, two or three years duration should be given for this.

The course of formation will be beneficial if the candidate, while evaluating herself with respect to the vocational features proper to this form of consecrated life, progressively acquires the necessary freedom to be educated and formed each day by experience. It should allow her to deepen her knowledge of her own resources and limits, of her capacity to counter resistance or to facilitate her conformity to the action of the Holy Spirit and, in every existential situation, to learn to gather the fragments of truth, beauty and goodness in which the grace of God is present and operative. This fundamental attitude of facing reality with attention, intelligence and a sense of responsibility, aroused and motivated by the desire to grow in the love of Christ, will lead to the maturation of her committed willingness to proceed with ongoing formative obligations after she receives consecration.

98. The obligation of the Bishop, the Delegate and the consecrated women who collaborate in the service of formation will therefore consist in ensuring that the candidate receives a systematic introduction to the charism and to the features of this form of life, in accompanying her while she intensifies and deepens her spiritual life and in observing how she harmonizes and arranges her lifestyle in docility to the action of the Spirit. In this way, they will collect the necessary elements for the definitive discernment about her admission to consecration.

Frequent and regular meetings with the spiritual director will be a valuable help to the candidate for her growth in the capacity to discern the plans of God, to integrate the formative elements in a wise synthesis, and to interpret in the light of faith the different experiences of her life: prayer, work, relationships and ecclesial service, family relationships, friendships, study and cultural enrichment, charitable and social obligations, experience of her own limits and fragility, ascetical commitments, etc.

99. It is important that the candidate be accompanied as she establishes a regular, constant pattern of prayer, with participation, daily if possible, at the Eucharist, the celebration of the Liturgy of the Hours, or at least Lauds and Vespers, mediation on the sacred Scriptures and devotion to Mary. The goal, above all, is to help her to consolidate her love for prayer and to develop her capacity to manage the rhythms of the day, the week and the year, so as to safeguard the centrality of the experience of dialogue with the Lord[100].

100. Since this form of consecrated life is inserted in the particular Church, the candidate will nurture her bonds with the ecclesial community, by means of the network of fraternal relationships that make up the ordinary fabric of daily ecclesial life, and also,

[100] Congregation for Institutes of Consecrated Life and Societies of Apostolic Life, Instruction *Starting afresh from Christ. A renewed commitment to consecrated life in the third millennium* (19 May 2002), 25.

when possible, by participating in significant diocesan events.

To strengthen her link with the particular Church, it is appropriate for the candidate to acquire adequate knowledge of its history, institutions, spiritual traditions, current pastoral activities and prophetic experiences as well as the difficulties that must be faced and the wounds that cause suffering.

Depending on each one's aptitudes, resources and charisms, the responsibility to build up the community can be expressed in pastoral service or in another form of witness that expresses her participation in the evangelizing mission and the human promotion of the Church, in the social and cultural context in which she lives.

101. For a correct understanding of the *Ordo virginum*, the candidate will be invited to study and reflect on the history of consecrated life and its value as a prophetic sign in the Church and in the world, starting with the foundational texts: the sacred Scriptures, the patristic tradition and theological reflection, with particular reference to Vatican Council II and to recent documents of the Church's magisterium.

The theological, liturgical, ecclesiological and juridical foundations of the life of the

Ordo virginum will be presented in detail, introducing the candidate to a deep understanding of the rite of consecration of virgins, its dynamic structure and its ecclesial significance.

102. An adequate knowledge and assimilation of the foundations of Christian anthropology must be offered, so that the choice of consecration will mature on the basis of a balanced understanding of human sexuality and affectivity, relationality and freedom, self-giving, sacrifice and suffering. In this framework, in the formation process the contributions of human sciences can also be used, particularly psychology and pedagogy, to put the candidate in a position to better understand relational dynamics and human development, and thus her own personal history and her way of relating to others.

When her practical circumstances and her personal abilities allow, the candidate will be encouraged to attend courses of study at theological colleges, institutes of religious science or similar institutions. In no case should an adequate theological preparation in the areas of biblical studies, liturgy, spirituality, ecclesiology and moral theology be omitted

103. Opportunities for instruction, formation and sharing of experience with the other candidates and consecrated women in the Diocese will be encouraged. If there are no others, the possibility will be explored of establishing connections for instruction and fraternal sharing with consecrated women or candidates in neighbouring Dioceses.

Admission to consecration and arrangements for the celebration

104. At the end of the formation course as agreed with the Bishop, after a careful discernment, both personally and with the spiritual accompanier, the candidate will present her request for admission to the Bishop. It is appropriate that this request be written in her own hand and that it mentions the recommendation of the spiritual accompanier.

The Bishop then takes up the responsibility of the definitive discernment. For this purpose, he will collect the necessary information from all those who have accompanied the journey of the candidate, excluding her spiritual accompanier. In particular, he must ask for the opinion of the Delegate, if he has appointed one, with the reasons on which the opinion is based, concerning the question of admission. The consecrated women who have been involved in the service of formation contribute to the preparation of this opinion.

105. Admission to consecration requires moral certainty about the authenticity of the candidate's vocation, the real existence of a virginal charism and the presence of the conditions and prerequisites for the candidate to accept and respond to the grace of consecration, and be able to bear eloquent witness of her own vocation, persevering in it and growing in generous self-giving to the Lord and to her neighbour.

106. If the assessment leads to her admission to consecration, the Bishop, with the one to be consecrated, will determine the date and the place of its celebration, keeping in mind the relevant guidelines in the Pontifical.

It is appropriate to arrange for the community to participate profitably in the liturgy of consecration, with an invitation to accompany the one to be consecrated in prayer and with a specific catechesis on the characteristics of this vocation. In the preparation and celebration of the rite, care is to be taken to introduce the assembly to the nuptial mystery of Christ and the Church that is to be celebrated, through the dignity and restraint of the gestures, hymns and recommended symbols.

107. After the celebration has taken place it will be documented with an entry in the register of the *Ordo virginum*, adding the personal signature of the celebrating minister, the consecrated woman herself and two witnesses. This register is ordinarily safeguarded in the diocesan curia. A certificate of the event will be issued to the consecrated woman. It is also appropriate for the Bishop to make arrangements to inform the competent parish priest about the consecration so that it can be annotated in the baptismal register.

Permanent formation

Attention to permanent formation

108. Concern for permanent formation is based on the need to respond more fully to the vocation received[101].

It requires constant openness to learning from experience, the disposition to let herself be led by the Spirit in the dynamism of

[101] Congregation for Institutes of Consecrated Life and Societies of Apostolic Life, Instruction *Starting afresh from Christ. A renewed commitment to consecrated life in the third millennium* (19 May 2002), 15.

faith, developing the meaning of the different stages of her life in the light of the Gospel and her own way of accounting for Christian hope in the face of the pressures of contemporary culture.

Increasing age, which is accompanied by changes in commitments, relational contexts and health conditions, impels consecrated women to rediscover the beauty and fertility of their consecration throughout all stages of life, appropriately adapting the content and manner of their formation.

All the dimensions of the life of the consecrated woman must be involved: her identity as a woman in a specific cultural and social context, a disciple of the Lord in the pilgrim Church in history, called to be a special sign of the spousal love of Christ and the Church, as a consecrated woman in the specific form of life of the *Ordo virginum*.

109. Permanent formation therefore requires humility, attention, intelligence, responsibility and creativity on the part of each consecrated woman.

In this context, the specific activities of permanent formation are instruments intended to help deepen their personal understanding of the virginal charism, to foster the integration of living in total dedication to the Lord, and to sustain the consecrated women in their commitment to fulfil the responsibilities that arise from consecration.

Personal commitment and the communal dimension

110. The preparation of useful programs of permanent formation requires harmonization of the personal commitment to formation with the communal dimension that characterize the *Ordo virginum.*

It concerns a choice of the priorities and most suitable means for a solid formation, so that it is attentive to the needs and the charisms of each one. At the same time, the formation programs must express and support the experience of communion that unites the consecrated women of the *Ordo virginum.*

This entails a dual exercise of co-responsibility: of each consecrated woman in relation to the Bishop or the Delegate, to plan and evaluate how she is fulfilling her commitment to formation; and of the group of consecrated women of the Diocese with the Bishop or the Delegate, to plan, implement and evaluate a shared, specific program of formation for the consecrated women of the *Ordo virginum.*

111. For this second aspect, depending on the circumstances, the Bishop or the Delegate will encourage meetings and formative activities for all the consecrated women, welcoming the contribution that each one is able to give in the planning, organization, implementation and the necessary evaluation. To give continuity and structure to this exercise of co-responsibility, the Bishop can arrange with the consecrated women the manner of establishing a service or team for permanent formation, as an expression of the service of communion.

Care must be taken to provide for the involvement of those consecrated women who are not able to, or have difficulty in participating in formation meetings because of advanced age, health or other serious reasons.

Where there is only one consecrated woman in a Diocese, or their number is very small, shared formation activities can be provided with the consecrated women of neighbouring Dioceses, with the agreement of the respective Bishops.

The consecrated women can also consider other initiatives and activities available in the Christian community for their own formation, and they can take advantage of suitable formative opportunities offered in their social and work environment.

Recommendations for content and method

112. Special formative programs for the consecrated women in the *Ordo virginum* must be designed with pedagogical expertise. They will consist of in-depth study of the fundamental themes of Christian life, particularly those more central to this form of consecrated life, and also reflection on questions raised by current reality which require serious evangelical discernment.

These programs will include study of sacred scripture, theology and the dynamics of the spiritual life, as well as attention to the magisterium and the pastoral directions of the diocesan Bishop and the Holy Father.

It is important that the intellectual dimension of formation is not isolated, but integrated into the growth of life according to the Spirit, and continually stimulated and assessed with respect to the capacity to establish and maintain friendly relationships.

Care must therefore be taken that meetings and formative activities become opportunities for true communion in faith and mutual support for the consecrated women. The formation program will also be supported with communal prayer. The pedagogical dimension will not be neglected regarding the relational dynamics existing within the

Ordo virginum, encouraging hospitality and mutual respect, kindness and the intelligent management of tensions and conflicts that arise, so that these also become occasions for growth.

113. Formative meetings and activities can take the form of lectures and conferences, sharing of experience, listening to testimony, shared reading courses, seminars, retreats, spiritual exercises, Bible study weeks, pilgrimages, cultural enrichment, etc.

Diocesan formation programs can be supplemented by inter-diocesan formation meetings and activities, particularly those organized by services of communion permanently established within a definite group of particular Churches, with the agreement of the relevant episcopal conferences and the Bishops' representative for the *Ordo virginum*, if one has been appointed. In the planning, implementation and assessment of these events the co-responsibility of all the consecrated women of these Dioceses must be encouraged.

CONCLUSION

114. The Lord Jesus drew all peoples into one Church and united them mystically with spousal love. This wonderful mystery, which is brought about efficaciously in the Eucharistic celebration, is the principle of the Church's unity and holiness, its universal mission and its ability to enliven all human experience and every culture with the message of the Gospel. Contemplating this mystery, the Church recognises the revival of the *Ordo virginum* as a gift of the Spirit and welcomes it with gratitude.

Preceded and sustained by the grace of God, the women who receive this consecration are called to live in obedience to the Holy Spirit, to experience the transforming energy of the Word of God that brings so many different women into a communion of sisters, and to proclaim the Gospel of salvation with their words and their lives, becoming images of the Church as the Bride, living only for Christ the Bridegroom, and thus making Him present to the world.

They look to Mary, perfect image of the Church, as the guiding star for their journey. The Church entrusts them to her maternal protection.

115. We praise you,
Virgin Mother of God
Woman of the covenant,
of expectation and fulfilment.
Be the mother and teacher
of consecrated virgins,
so that imitating you
they will receive the Gospel joyfully
and every day
with humility and wonder
discover in it
the holy origin
of their spousal vocation.

Virgin of virgins,
sealed fountain,
gate of heaven,
inspire and accompany
these sisters of ours,
may they have the gift
of spiritual discernment
pilgrims in history
may they live the dynamism
of prophecy
with freedom and courage
with determination and tenderness.

Woman full of grace,
overflowing with charity,
Virgin become Church
bless their journey
so that hope
enlightens their minds
and opens their hearts
guiding every step
and faith
makes their hands industrious
and creative
so may their lives be fruitful
and anticipating here and now
the reality of the Kingdom,
may they generate
and build up the people of God
sharing in its mission
kingly, prophetic and priestly.

We proclaim you blessed
woman of the Magnificat
mother of the living Gospel.
We pray for these sisters.
Gather them in your song
involve them in your dance
so that they follow the Lamb
wherever he goes
with lamps alight.
May they lead us also
to the eternal wedding banquet,

to the final embrace
with the Love
that never ends.

(*Approved by the Holy Father*
in an audience on June 8, 2018)

Vatican City, June 8, 2018
Solemnity the Most Sacred Heart of Jesus

João Braz Card. de Aviz
Prefect

✠ José Rodríguez Carballo, O.F.M.
Archbishop Secretary

INDEX

www.ingramcontent.com/pod-product-compliance
Ingram Content Group UK Ltd.
Pitfield, Milton Keynes, MK11 3LW, UK
UKHW040003200726
13854UKWH00001B/14